NORTHUMBRIA

ENGLISH BORDER COUNTRY

NORTHUMBRIA

ENGLISH BORDER COUNTRY

PHOTOGRAPHS BY ROB TALBOT

TEXT BY ROBIN WHITEMAN

WEIDENFELD & NICOLSON
LONDON

First published in Great Britain in 1998
by Weidenfeld & Nicolson

A CIP catalogue record for this book is available
from the British Library
ISBN 0 297 82249 7

Designed by: Harry Green
Map Created By: Technical Art Services
Printed and Bound in: Italy
Set in: Bembo

Weidenfeld & Nicolson
The Orion Publishing Group Ltd
Orion House
5 Upper Saint Martin's Lane
London WC2H 9EA

HALF-TITLE PAGE: ST CUTHBERT'S CAVE, KYLOE HILLS

In the remote and wooded Kyloe Hills, near Holburn Grange, five kms (three miles) west of Belford, is a natural sandstone cave reputed to be one of the places where the body of St Cuthbert rested on its 120-year-long journey from Lindisfarne to Durham. Alternatively, some believe the cave may have been used as a hermitage by the saint himself. In *The Life and Miracles of St Cuthbert*, Bede wrote: 'For his first introduction to the solitary life, he withdrew to the quietest spot outside the monastery walls [at Lindisfarne]. But, after spending some time in this solitude, fighting the invisible adversary with prayer and fasting, he decided to set himself a greater challenge by seeking out a place of combat that was more remote and more distant from the eyes of men.' The place he finally chose was, of course, the Inner Farne. Local legend says that 'Cuddy's Cave' is haunted by the restless ghost of a reiver who buried his booty nearby, but cannot remember where. Both it and the surrounding woodland are now the property of the National Trust.

TITLE PAGE: CRAG LOUGH, NEAR HOUSESTEADS

Lying at the foot of the steep dolerite escarpment which once formed part of the northern frontier of Roman Britain, Crag Lough is the smallest of several lakes to be found in the area around Housesteads. In addition to being a haven for wildlife, supporting a rich variety of vegetation from yellow water-lilies to thickets of willow 'carr', the shallow lake is popular with trout fishermen. The near-vertical walls of rock (known as Highshield Crags) are a magnet for rock climbers, whilst the stretch of footpath running along the top of the ridge is shared by walkers of both the Pennine Way and Hadrian's Wall. In 1947, the government-appointed Hobhouse Committee recommended the setting up of certain National Parks, including Northumberland. Their report contained the following: 'To stand on the Roman Wall above Crag Lough...is to see the hills and wild moorland very much as they must have looked to the soldiers of the Roman Empire who for nearly 300 years mounted guard over the civilisation that lay behind them.'

ENDPAPERS: ROCK FACES NEAR ARMATHWAITE

CONTENTS

ACKNOWLEDGEMENTS

Robin Whiteman and Rob Talbot would particularly like to acknowledge the generous co-operation of English Heritage (Historic Properties North), and the National Trust Regional Office of Northumbria for allowing them to take photographs of their properties and sites featured in this book. They are also extremely grateful for photographic permissions from the following: Christopher & Sally Nightingale (Appleby Castle); T. H. Baker-Cresswell (Preston Tower); Sir Humphry Wakefield Bt. (Chillingham Castle); Robin Birley on behalf of the Vindolanda Trust; Cumbria County Council (Birdoswald Roman Fort); Tyne and Wear Museums (Arbeia Roman Fort); and the Arts, Libraries & Museums Department of Durham County Council (Killhope Lead Mining Centre). A special thanks to Stan Beckensall (authority on Northumbrian prehistoric rock art) and Ian Parnall of Shankhead Farm. Appreciation also extends to all those individuals and organizations too numerous to mention by name who nevertheless have made such a valuable contribution.

OTHER BOOKS BY ROB TALBOT AND ROBIN WHITEMAN

THE COTSWOLDS

THE ENGLISH LAKES

THE YORKSHIRE MOORS & DALES

THE HEART OF ENGLAND

THE WEST COUNTRY

WESSEX

THE GARDEN OF ENGLAND

EAST ANGLIA & THE FENS

THE PEAK DISTRICT

CADFAEL COUNTRY

BROTHER CADFAEL'S HERB GARDEN

SHAKESPEARE'S AVON

ENGLISH LANDSCAPES

LAKELAND LANDSCAPES

YORKSHIRE LANDSCAPES

Photographs by Rob Talbot

SHAKESPEARE COUNTRY

THE LAKELAND POETS

COTSWOLD VILLAGES

Text by Robin Whiteman

THE CADFAEL COMPANION

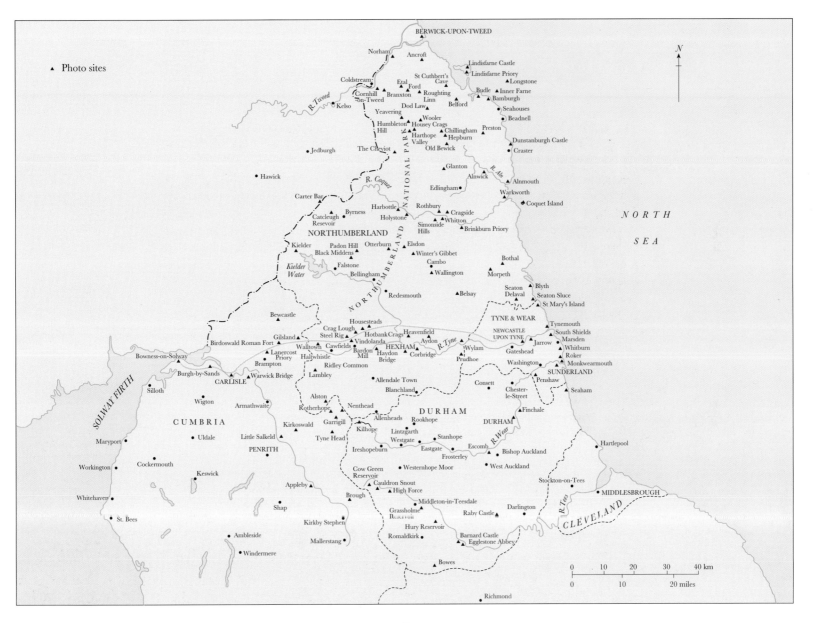

▲ Photo sites

BERWICK-UPON-TWEED

Norham
Ancroft
Lindisfarne Castle
Lindisfarne Priory
Coldstream
St Cuthbert's Cave
Longstone
Etal Ford
Budle Inner Farne
Cornhill -on-Tweed
Branxton
Roughting Linn
Bamburgh
Kelso
Dod Law
Belford
Seahouses
Yeavering
Beadnell
Wooler
Housey Crags
Preston
Humbleton Hill
Chillingham
Harthope Valley
Hepburn
Dunstanburgh Castle
Old Bewick
Craster
Jedburgh
The Cheviot
Glanter
R. Alm
Hawick
Alnwick
Alnmouth
Edlingham
Warkworth
Carter Bar
R. Coquet
Coquet Island
Harbottle
Rothbury
Byrness
Cragside
Catcleugh Resevoir
Holystone
Whitton
NORTH
Simonside Hills
Brinkburn Priory
SEA
NORTHUMBERLAND
Kielder
Padon Hill
Otterburn
Elsdon
Black Middens
Winter's Gibbet
Bothal
Kielder Water
Falstone
Cambo
Morpeth
Bellingham
Wallington
Blyth
Seaton Delaval
Seaton Sluce
Redesmouth
Belsay
St Mary's Island
Bewcastle
Housesteads
TYNE & WEAR
Crag Lough
Heavenfield
Tynemouth
Gilsland
Steel Rig
Hotbank Crags
NEWCASTLE UPON TYNE
South Shields
Birdoswald Roman Fort
Walltown
Vindolanda
Aydon
Marsden
Cawfields
HEXHAM
Jarrow
Bowness-on-Solway
Lanercost Priory
Bardon Mill
Haydon Bridge
Corbridge
R. Tyne
Wylam
Gateshead
Whitburn
Roker
Haltwhistle
Prudhoe
Washington
Monkwearmouth
Brampton
Ridley Common
SUNDERLAND
Burgh-by-Sands
Warwick Bridge
Lambley
Allendale Town
Consett
Penshaw
CARLISLE
Blanchland
Chester-le-Street
Seaham
Silloth
Alston
Finchale
Wigton
Rotherhope
Nenthead
DURHAM
Armathwaite
Allenheads
Rookhope
DURHAM
Kirkoswald
Garrigill
Lintzgarth
Maryport
Little Salkeld
Killhope
Westgate
Stanhope
Escomb
Bishop Auckland
Hartlepool
Uldale
Tyne Head
Ireshopeburn
Eastgate
PENRITH
Frosterley
Cow Green Reservoir
Westernhope Moor
West Auckland
Workington
Cockermouth
Keswick
Cauldron Snout
Stockton-on-Tees
Whitehaven
Appleby
High Force
Middleton-in-Teesdale
MIDDLESBROUGH
St. Bees
Shap
Brough
Grassholme Reservoir
Darlington
Raby Castle
CLEVELAND
Kirkby Stephen
Hury Reservoir
Ambleside
Mallerstang
Romaldkirk
Barnard Castle
Egglestone Abbey
Windermere
Bowes
Richmond

CUMBRIA

SOLWAY FIRTH

R. Tweed

R. Wear

R. Tees

0   10   20   30   40 km
0   10   20 miles

INTRODUCTION

࿐

HAYDON BRIDGE

During medieval times, when peace was short-lived and warfare flourished, the vital route across the River South Tyne at Haydon Bridge was often used by both Scottish and English marauders. To try and control the movement of undesirable traffic across the bridge, therefore, it was frequently barred and chained. The old bridge was washed away by the great flood of 1771. Its replacement underwent major repairs after further flood damage in the early nineteenth century. In 1824, it was recorded that the present six-arch bridge had been 'very recently widened and thoroughly repaired'. It is now restricted to pedestrians. The new road bridge nearby was constructed in 1970. Haydon Bridge is noted for being the childhood home of the painter, John Martin, who was born at East Land Ends, south of the river, in 1789. While young Martin was sketching with a stick in the smooth sand along the riverside, he may well have seen the town's celebrated eccentric, Ned Coulson, running along the road whilst playing a violin behind his back.

No region in England, not even the once-turbulent border with Wales, has witnessed so many centuries of ungovernable violence, tragedy and lawlessness as the English Border Country of Northumbria. Even the might of the Roman army was unable to pacify the land entirely, settling instead to define the north-westernmost boundary of the Roman Empire by building a great wall (named after the Emperor Hadrian) from one side of the coast to the other. During the so-called 'Dark Ages', Britons fought against Anglo-Saxons, kings against kings, and Christians against pagans. Viking raids on coastal monasteries and settlements followed, plunging the countryside into years of chaos and turmoil. With the Vikings came the end of the 'Golden Age' of Anglo-Saxon culture and learning, which flowered in Northumbria under the influence of monasteries like Lindisfarne and the dual-house of Jarrow and Wearmouth (Monkwearmouth). Christianity, once again, was eclipsed by paganism and idolatry.

The arrival of the Normans brought renewed outbreaks of violence and fighting, notably William the Conqueror's brutal scorched-earth policy of revenge against Northumbrian resistance, known as the 'harrowing of the north'. From medieval times up until the early seventeenth century, the Anglo-Scottish Borderlands were overrun by raiding gangs of outlaws and bandits (known as reivers) whose whole way of life was based on rustling, feuding amongst themselves, terrorism and blackmail. As the ordinary laws of England and Wales proved to be ineffective in this wild and stormy frontier – where the regulations of one country could be played off against those of the other – a separate Anglo-Scottish Border Law was created. This was meant to be enforced by the Wardens of the Marches and other Border officers. But, as many of the law-keepers were also reivers themselves, fair and impartial justice could not always be guaranteed. After the reivers came the mosstroopers – Border raiders who were particularly active during the seventeenth century.

Peace did not finally come to Northumbria until after the Jacobite rebellion of 1745, and the defeat of the army of Bonnie Prince Charlie at the battle of Culloden the following year. Determined to ensure that the Stuarts and their supporters would never rise up in rebellion again, the Hanoverian government brutally executed all those who had supported the Jacobite cause, then systematically set about crushing the highland clans: first by destroying their homes, and then by removing the power of their chieftains. The Stuart claim to the throne effectively ended when Bonnie Prince Charlie died abroad in 1788.

The Industrial Revolution of the late eighteenth and early nineteenth centuries transformed the north-east of England (the area east of Durham, between the mouths of the Tyne and the Tees) from a landscape and society that was predominantly rural to one that was predominantly urban. Major industries like coal mining, shipbuilding, engineering and iron-and-steel manufacturing flourished, turning the area into one of the great industrial centres of the world. One major contribution to the success and prosperity of the North-East was the development of the railway system, pioneered by the Northumbrian engineer, George Stephenson. It was George and his son, Robert, who designed and constructed the world's first steam-powered public railway – the Stockton and Darlington railway, opened in 1825.

After the First World War, fierce international competition brought a massive slump in industrial production, leading to closures, unemployment and poverty in the North-East on an unprecedented scale. Today, shipbuilding, coal mining and heavy engineering in the area have been replaced by lighter industries, as well as by the huge chemical plants and oil refineries around Teesside.

Despite its rich industrial and railway heritage, however, Northumbria is also a land of wide open spaces and far horizons – where often the only sounds to be heard are the haunting cry of the curlew or the challenging call of the grouse. Occupying the heart of the region is the Northumberland National Park, designated in 1956 and covering an area of 1,030 square kms (398 square miles). From Hadrian's Wall, the Park stretches north towards the Anglo-Scottish border for some seventy kms (forty-five miles) to end near Wooler in the valleys of the River Glen and Bowmont Water. Within the Park the landscape is dominated by hills that rise in height, through farming dales and heather moorland, to the Cheviots – the highest point of which is the Cheviot at 2,676 feet (816 metres) above sea-level. Like every other National Park in England and Wales, nearly all the land is in private, rather than public, ownership. The largest landowner in the Northumberland National Park is the Ministry of Defence with over one-fifth of the total area, followed by the Forestry Commission with only slightly less. Between Coquetdale and Redesdale is a Ministry of Defence training area, part of which is a live firing range where public access is restricted.

England's largest reservoir, Kielder Water – located within Britain's largest forest – lies just outside the western boundary of the Park. Running along the southern edge of the Park and providing the natural foundations for a substantial section of Hadrian's Wall is the Great Whin Sill. Formed of hard molten basalt or dolerite, this famous geological outcrop stretches (with a few breaks) north-eastward for over 100 kms (sixty miles), from near the source of the River South Tyne to the coastal fortresses of Dunstanburgh and Bamburgh. Offshore it forms the dominant rock of the Farne Islands: noted for their large colonies of seabirds and for being the scene of Grace Darling's heroic sea rescue. To the south of the National Park are the North Pennines, which effectively act as a north–south dividing line, separating the predominantly agricultural countryside around Carlisle and the Vale of Eden in the west, from the predominantly industrial landscape of Tyne, Wear and Tees in the east. Threading a meandering route up the North Pennines, along Hadrian's Wall and over the Cheviots is the northern section of the 435-km (270-mile) Pennine Way, running from Edale in the Peak District to the Scottish village of Kirk Yetholm, just over the border. North of the bustling city and commercial centre of Newcastle-upon-Tyne, and east of the Northumberland National Park, the scenery becomes increasingly rural until farms, fields and pastures cover the low, undulating hills, with a living patchwork of greens, yellows and browns, and coal-blackened shores are transformed into miles of golden sands.

As the history of Northumbria is essentially the story of ceaseless wars, bitter feuds and bloody battles, it is not surprising that the traditional architecture of the region is the fortified dwelling – the castle, the pele tower and the bastle house. Indeed, as it contains more strongholds than any other region in Britain, Northumberland has been described as 'England's castle county *par excellence*'. To protect themselves from attack, particularly after the Scottish victory over the English at Bannockburn in 1314, all who could afford it made sure they lived in some form of fortified or defensible building: the nobility in their castles, the lesser gentry in their pele towers and the farmers in their bastle houses. Those too poor to build stone strongholds built dwellings that could be re-erected very quickly once destroyed in a raid.

Even after the union of the crowns of Scotland and England under James VI and I, when large mansions were being built further south, the wealthy landowners of Northumberland were forced to retain defence as the main priority in any improvements to their homes. Even today, at the heart of most large houses in the Northumbrian countryside lies some form of fortified structure: the few exceptions being mansions erected after peace finally came to the region in the late eighteenth century. Increasing stability and prosperity also brought about a spate of church building, in which many ruinous structures were replaced by new ones. The earliest nonconformist building in Northumbria was the Presbyterian church at Morpeth, built in 1722. Chapels for Methodists, Quakers, Baptists and other nonconformists followed.

One important legacy of prolonged Border strife in the region is the rich treasury of tales and ballads, which record the bloody deeds and savage way of life of reiving families, such as the Armstrongs, Charltons, Elliots and Grahams. Many of these old ballads were collected and preserved (and often embellished) by Sir Walter Scott (1771–1832), who was fascinated by the history of his native Scotland and the Borders. They appeared in the three-volume *Minstrelsy of the Scottish Border*, published in 1802–3, which undoubtedly inspired his original work, the romantic poem *The Lay of the Last Minstrel* (1805). He also used his knowledge of the Northumbrian people and landscape in his poem *Marmion* (1808) and his novels *Guy Mannering* (1815) and *Rob Roy* (1817). The rebel-rousing story of the Scottish folk hero and freedom fighter, William Wallace (eventually executed by Edward I in 1305), was recently retold in the film *Braveheart*, starring Mel Gibson. Other far more ancient Northumbrian legends and traditions include numerous accounts of ogres, demons and dragons, and several stories of hideous 'worm' monsters, which ravaged the countryside killing animals and children. The struggle of Christianity against paganism, during the Anglo-Saxon and Viking Ages, produced many stories of miracles, martyrdom and saintly deeds, some of which were documented by the Venerable Bede of Jarrow monastery.

Although the ancient kingdom of Northumbria stretched from the Firth of Forth in the north to the Humber in the south, for the purpose of this book the region extends south from the present Anglo-Scottish border to include the geographical territories of Northumberland, north and east Cumbria, Durham, Cleveland and Tyne and Wear. The regions immediately to the south of this 'English Border Country' are covered by the 'Country Series' companion volumes: *The English Lakes* and *The Yorkshire Moors & Dales*.

In the early eighteenth century, Daniel Defoe wrote of Northumberland in *A Tour Thro' the Whole Island of Great Britain*:

> Here is abundant business for an antiquary; every place shows you ruined castles, Roman altars, inscriptions, monuments of battle, of heroes killed, and armies routed, and the like: The towns of Morpeth, Alnwick, Warkworth, Tickill, and many others, show their old castles, and some of them still in tolerable repair, as Alnwick in particular, and Warkworth; others, as Bamburgh, Norham, Chillingham, Horton, Dunstar, Wark, and innumerable more, are sunk in their own ruins, by the mere length of time.

From Berwick-upon-Tweed, England's northernmost town, to the distinctly different valleys of the Eden, Wear and Tees, and the historic cities of Carlisle, Durham and Newcastle-upon-Tyne, Northumbria is a land of surprising contrasts and constant surprises.

BLACK HILL & WEARDALE, FROM WESTERNHOPE MOOR

Rising on the 2,113-foot (644-metre) high watershed of Slate Hill – between Killhope and Nenthead – the River Wear flows south-eastward to Bishop Auckland, before meandering north-eastward, past Durham, Chester-le-Street and Washington, to debouch into the North Sea at Sunderland. During medieval times, the area between the hamlets of Eastgate and Westgate in upper Weardale was the hunting preserve of the Prince Bishops of Durham. During their 'Great Chases', which were conducted with much pomp and pageantry, the inhabitants of the valley were not only required to provide hounds for the hunt and food for the hunters, they were also expected to help in the construction of temporary buildings, including a large hall and chapel. Those caught poaching were severely punished. In 1818 some lead miners were caught shooting grouse and taken to Stanhope, to await transportation to Durham gaol. In the 'battle' that followed the men were freed. The inn in which they were held captive was appropriately renamed the 'Bonny Moor Hen'.

HEXHAM & THE CENTRAL BORDER

ॐ

*HADRIAN'S WALL,
FROM HOTBANK CRAGS*

Stretching 120 kms (seventy-three miles), or eighty Roman miles, coast to coast across the narrowest part of northern England – from Wallsend on the River Tyne in the east to Bowness-on-Solway in the west – Hadrian's Wall was largely completed by AD 130. Named after the emperor who ordered its const-ruction in 122, it was originally three metres (nine feet) wide and up to six metres (twenty feet) high, including a parapet to the north. At every Roman mile along its length, the builders – mostly legionaries – constructed a small guard post, or milecastle. A turret, sited every third of a Roman mile between each milecastle, served as a signal or lookout post. Shortly after Hadrian's death in 138 his successor, the Emperor Antonius Pius, ordered the construction of a new wall almost 160 kms (100 miles) further north. Known as the Antonine Wall, it was abandoned in about 162, leaving Hadrian's Wall – with its formidable series of defensive ditches and mounds – the north-western frontier of the Roman Empire until the final withdrawal of the legions from Britain in 410.

Despite its close proximity to Hadrian's Wall and the presence of large quantities of Roman stone in its older buildings, there is no evidence to substantiate claims that the ancient market town of Hexham was the site of a Roman station. However, amongst the Roman relics preserved inside Hexham Abbey is the impressive tombstone of Flavinus, a standard bearer of the *Ala Petriana* cavalry unit. The inscription records that the soldier had completed seven years' service before his death at the age of twenty-five. From the style of the lettering and the dress of the fully uniformed warrior, the stone has been dated to the late first century AD. Like many other Roman stones in the Abbey, it is thought to have been brought from the military fort and garrison town at Corbridge, only five kms (three miles) from Hexham down the River Tyne.

The earliest fort at Corbridge dates from about AD 79 – around the time when all of England and Wales was finally brought under Roman control. Although the legions, under Julius Caesar, first invaded the island in 55 BC, and again in 54 BC, it was not until AD 43 that the Roman conquest of Britain began in earnest. After crossing the Channel, the legions landed unopposed on the shores of south-east Britain and, despite encountering fierce resis-tance inland, rapidly subjugated the tribes of lowland England. Many of the British, or Celtic, aristocracy, aware of the life-style and material comforts enjoyed by their conquered counter-parts on the Continent, readily swore allegiance to Rome and were absorbed into the culture and society of the new Roman province. Others rebelled, like Caradoc, or Caratacus, (leader of the Silures of south Wales and later the Ordovices of central Wales) and Boudicca, or Boadicea, (queen of the Iceni tribe of East Anglia). Boudicca, defeated at a decisive battle in the Midlands, died either by suicide or from illness, while Caradoc was handed over to the Romans by Cartimanua, queen of the Brigantes of northern England, into whose territory he had fled hoping for safe refuge. It is thought that Cartimanua's capital stronghold was at Stanwick, ten kms (six miles) north of Richmond.

If Cartimanua was pro-Roman, her husband, Venutius, was totally the opposite. After she had divorced him for another man, Venutius decided to challenge her right to power. By

AD 71 he was the undisputed ruler of the Brigantian kingdom and an open enemy of Rome. For the Romans, conquest of the Brigantes was the only solution. A major obstacle in their way was the natural barrier formed by the bleak Pennine terrain. The Roman army, under Petillius Cerialis, decided to mount their long, hard military campaigns from the eastern side of the hills, from the newly established legionary fortress of *Eboracum* (York). To complete the strategy, the forces under Julius Agricola advanced up the western side of the country to create a pincer movement on the southern Pennines. Control of the cross-Pennine route over the Stainmore Pass – linking the Eden Valley in the west to the Vale of York in the east – was established by a series of marching camps and garrison forts along a military highway.

Information on Cerialis' victory over Venutius is obscure, nor is it known whether the Briton was defeated in a final battle. But, after the loss of their leader, Brigantian opposition quickly crumbled. Reduced to relatively small tribal units, rather than a large coordinated fighting force, the rebels were effectively beaten, but not conquered. Not yet. For in AD 78 the Romans, under Agricola – newly appointed governor of Britain – turned their attention to consolidating their hold on North Wales.

Once this had been accomplished, the army pushed northward from the legionary fortress of *Deva* (Chester) up the western side of the Pennines and by the end of AD 79 they controlled not only the territory of the Brigantes, but also that of the Carvetii (around Carlisle and the Eden Valley). Agricola's ambition, however, was to conquer the whole of island Britain and to this end he wasted no time in advancing into Scotland as far north as the River Tay. The two main routes north into Scotland were from Corbridge in the east and Carlisle in the west; at both places Agricola built military forts. In AD 81 he established a fortified frontier across the Forth–Clyde isthmus and, three years later, decisively defeated the Caledonii at the battle of *Mons Graupius*. New roads were subsequently built to control the newly won territories. These included Dere Street (running north from York, through Corbridge, to Scotland) and the Stanegate road (linking Corbridge and Carlisle).

Hostility to the Romans in western Scotland exploded after AD 87 when the Romans' military presence was weakened by the withdrawal of troops from Britain to quell troubles elsewhere in the Empire. The Forth–Clyde frontier was abandoned and a new frontier created on the Tyne–Solway isthmus (the line of the Stanegate road). In 122 the Emperor Hadrian visited Britain and ordered the construction of a wall right across the isthmus, from Wallsend in the east to Bowness-on-Solway in the west. The original plan was not to build forts on the Wall itself, but to station army units to the south of it. Nor was it planned to construct the Vallum, the great earthwork running along the entire 120-km (seventy-three-mile) length of the Wall.

Eastward from the point where the frontier crossed the River Irthing (near Gilsland), the Wall was built of stone. Westward it was built of turf. At mile intervals there were gates, each defended by a small guard post or milecastle. Between each pair of milecastles were two turrets or lookout posts. Whilst the work on Hadrian's northern frontier was still in progress, several modifications took place, including the addition of Wall forts and the Vallum. By about 130 the Wall was completed. It was patrolled and maintained not by legionary soldiers, but by well-trained auxiliary troops – Africans, Asians and Europeans from the non-Roman tribes of the Empire, many of whom hoped to live long enough to be granted Roman citizenship on their retirement from the army.

After Hadrian's death in 138, his successor, the Emperor Antonius Pius, decided to retake the lowlands of Scotland. Despite managing to move the frontier almost 160 kms (100 miles) further north – consolidated by a new wall called the Antonine Wall – the Romans were unable to reconquer the tribal territory of the Caledonii, further north. Nor were they able to maintain a permanent hold on the new frontier. For, in about 162, the Antonine Wall was abandoned, leaving Hadrian's Wall the north-westernmost limit of the Roman Empire for the next two hundred and fifty or so years.

After the Roman withdrawal from Britain, the Wall and its attendant fortifications gradually fell into ruin and much of the stone was recycled as building material, including many stones bearing carvings and/or inscriptions. Archaeological excavations along the frontier have unearthed valuable information on the people who lived and died at the northern extremity of military control in Roman Britain. The discoveries at the Stanegate fort and civil settlement of *Vindolanda* (Chesterholm) have been particularly outstanding. These include wooden writing tablets bearing texts ranging from an invitation to a birthday party to a letter recording the dispatch of a parcel containing socks, shoes and underpants.

In 1725, whilst digging foundations to strengthen the tower at Hexham Abbey, workmen accidentally rediscovered the Anglo-Saxon crypt (last recorded in the twelfth century), its walls built entirely of reused Roman stone. The reason why so many inscriptions face outward is due to their use by the builders as a key to which plaster could be applied to the walls. Yet, despite its wealth of Roman monuments, the known history of Hexham, like many other places in Northumbria, stems from the next significant development after the conquest – the arrival of Christianity in Britain.

VINDOLANDA ROMAN FORT

The Roman site of *Vindolanda* (Chesterholm), near Bardon Mill, contains the remains of several forts – the earliest, built of turf and timber, dating from around AD 85. Standing on the Stanegate road, the first northern frontier of Roman Britain, the fort was temporarily abandoned after the construction of Hadrian's Wall, a mile to the north. In about AD 160, the Romans built a new stone fort at *Vindolanda*, outside the walls of which a civil settlement developed and flourished. Incidentally, civilians lived at *Vindolanda* from the time the fort was first garrisoned. After its foundation in 1970, the Vindolanda Trust has undertaken extensive excavations of the site. Many of the outstanding finds, which include usually perishable and non-perishable items, are on display in the Chesterholm Museum. Of all the finds, the most important must be the wooden writing tablets, recording priceless information on Roman affairs. The site also contains reconstructions of a stone Wall with turret and a turf Wall with timber gateway.

HOUSESTEADS ROMAN FORT

Originally Hadrian's Wall was to have only milecastles and turrets, with forts to the south (like *Vindolanda*) to provide military reinforcement. Before its construction was completed, however, a decision was made to build a series of forts along the wall itself, on average some ten-and-a-half kms (six-and-a-half miles) apart. Each was to support a permanent garrison of soldiers (essentially auxiliary units, comprising between five hundred and a thousand mixed regiments of cavalry and infantry). Interestingly, Housesteads (*Vercovicium*) – the most famous and most complete example of a Wall fort – occupies the site of a demolished turret. Standing on the top of a high dolerite ridge overlooking the valley created by the Knag Burn, the five-acre fort is characteristically rectangular in shape with rounded corners (like playing cards). In addition to the granary, the floor of which was supported by stone piers (shown in the photograph), the site includes the remains of barrack rooms and a hospital. Evidence of the *vicus* (civilian settlement) can be seen outside the south gate.

HADRIAN'S WALL, FROM WALLTOWN CRAGS

Snaking along the top of Walltown Crags, north-east of Greenhead, is one of the best-preserved stretches of Hadrian's Wall, together with the remains of a turret (45a), originally built as a free-standing tower. Instead of being incorporated into the turret, the stones of the Wall simply butt up to its east and west sides. Stone for the construction of both the Wall and turret was quarried locally. Unfortunately, recent large-scale quarrying for whinstone has completely destroyed a section of the Wall to the east of the turret. Quarrying for stone pavings (and later chippings for road-making) started at Walltown in 1871 and ceased just over 100 years later. Today, Walltown Quarry has been transformed into a National Park recreation area, while five kms (three miles) east Cawfields (where the hillside has been cleanly sliced by quarrying) has been turned into a picnic area. The Roman fort and town of *Carvoran*, at the western end of Walltown Crags, is now the site of the Roman Army Museum. No trace of the ancient settlement of Walltown survives.

THE VALLUM, NEAR CAWFIELDS

In addition to Hadrian's Wall itself, with its regular series of milecastles, turrets and forts, the Romans constructed a V-shaped ditch to the north and the great earthwork ditch with its attendant mounds, known as the Vallum, to the south. Stretching along the entire length of the frontier from the Tyne to the Solway Firth, the Vallum ran on average some sixty-four metres (210 feet) from the Wall, its three-metre (ten feet) deep ditch being six metres (twenty feet) wide at the top, tapering to two-and-a-half metres (eight feet) at the bottom. Overall, the total width of the earthworks were some thirty-six metres (120 feet). Between the Wall and the Vallum a road (known as the Military Way) was constructed to facilitate the movement of soldiers and supplies. The Stanegate (or 'stone road') – the second of the two Roman roads which snaked east–west across the region – pre-dates the Wall, and ran from the fort of *Luguvalium* (Carlisle) to the fort of *Corstopitum* (Corbridge). Although the Stanegate was not a linear barrier, it was a vital (and defended) link in the road network of Roman Northumbria.

MILECASTLE 39 (CASTLE NICK), HADRIAN'S WALL

In *Northumberland & the Border* (1859) Walter White mused on Hadrian's Wall: 'What a contrast between the Rome that was, and the Britain that is! Christianity was but a spark known scarcely beyond the shores of the Mediterranean... How the sight of those old stones carries us back to the dawn of Christian history! When the legions were here fighting and building, they were within ninety years of the time when the Sermon on the Mount was preached; and but half a century from the death of St Paul and the destruction of Jerusalem. Here still prevailed the mysterious rites of the Druids, intermingled with a paganism tinctured with the wild mythology of the north...And when the wall was finished, we can imagine the alerts, the marchings to and fro, the relieving guard, the cries for signals, and rapid transmission of orders. Tradition once told of means for conveying signals, which, had it been true, would have been an anticipation of a modern contrivance; namely, that brass speaking tubes were laid all along the wall.'

HADRIAN'S WALL, NEAR CAWFIELDS

In 1801, at the age of seventy-eight, William Hutton walked over 965 kms (600 miles) from Birmingham and back 'to see a shattered Wall!' The account of his journey – the earliest record of anyone walking the whole length of Hadrian's Wall (or Severus's Wall, as he called it) – was published the following year in *The History of the Roman Wall, which crosses the Island of Britain from the German Ocean to the Irish Sea:* 'That man is born a savage, there needs no other proof than Severus's Wall. It characterizes two nations as robbers, and murderers...This Wall is a clear proof, that every species of cruelty that one man can practise on another was here, and pronounces the human being as much a savage as the brute. This place has been the scene of more plunder and murder than any part of the Island, of equal extent. During four hundred years, while the Wall continued a barrier, this was the grand theatre of war, as well as during ages after its destruction...This astonishing rampart...was designed to remedy the mischiefs described.'

STEEL HENGE, RIDLEY COMMON

Although there is abundant evidence of prehistoric settlement in Northumbria, including stone circles at Duddo, Hethpool and Little Salkeld (Long Meg & Her Daughters), not every monument is necessarily ancient. In spite of appearances, Steel Henge – a stone circle some five kms (three miles) south of Bardon Mill – was erected in the mid-1980s by Ian Parnall of Shankhead Farm. It takes its name from Steel Farm, which is close by. The stones have been correctly aligned to the summer and winter solstices – a process (using wooden stakes) which took ten frustrating years to achieve due to clouds persistently blocking the view of the rising sun at the crucial moments in time. The large stone, weighing over eight tons, bears the scars of the bulldozer which positioned it outside and to the east of the main circle. One day, perhaps, the marks may be interpreted as meaningful symbols. The twenty-three centimetre (nine-inch) lump missing from the stone on the south side of the circle was clandestinely chiselled off by German tourists eager to take home a genuine prehistoric souvenir!

LAMBLEY VIADUCT

From Haltwhistle, the Newcastle & Carlisle Railway Company built a branch line south to Alston to transport lead, coal and limestone from the workings on Alston Moor to Tyneside. Consisting of a single track, the line was opened in 1852. Near the village of Lambley, the trackbed was carried thirty-two metres (105 feet) over the River South Tyne by an impressive sixteen-arch sandstone viaduct, designed by the engineer, Sir George Barclay-Bruce. The stone came from quarries at Slaggyford (in the South Tyne Valley) and Bardon Mill (near Hexham). Nine of the arches span seventeen metres (fifty-six feet), and seven span six metres (twenty feet). The total length of the viaduct is 256 metres (840 feet). After the branch line closed in 1976, the condition of the viaduct deteriorated badly. It was restored in 1995–6 and is now in the care of the North Pennines Heritage Trust. Today, the sixteen-km (ten-mile) section between Featherstone and Alston (which includes Lambley Viaduct) forms the South Tyne Trail. However, part of the trackbed from Alston is also used by the narrow-gauge South Tynedale Railway.

THE CHANTRY & TELFORD BRIDGE, MORPETH

Although the main centre of the old market town of Morpeth developed on the north side of the Wansbeck, within a loop of the river, its parish church and castles were sited on the south side. Spanning the river, near the thirteenth-century Chantry of All Saints (now housing a Tourist Information Centre and Bagpipe Museum) and the Victorian United Reform Church of St George, are two bridges. These are the remains of the medieval Chantry bridge (Old Bridge), on the piers of which an iron and wood footbridge was erected in 1869, and Telford Bridge (New Bridge) completed in 1831. The earliest of Morpeth's two castles, a Norman motte-and-bailey castle, was erected on a hill in Carlisle Park, immediately south of the river. The other was built further south during the thirteenth century. Little remains of this castle today, apart from the fourteenth-century gatehouse. The parish church of St Mary, south-west of the gatehouse, is essentially fourteenth century. Since 1974 Morpeth has been the county town of Northumberland.

BOTHAL CASTLE

Five kms (three miles) east of Morpeth, Bothal Castle stands on a prominent hill overlooking the confluence of the River Wansbeck and its tributary, Brocks Burn. The name 'Bothal' may be derived from an Old English word meaning 'a dwelling or habitation', thereby indicating that there was a house (or houses) beside the river crossing – at least during Anglo-Saxon times. Standing on the site of an earlier fortification, the present castle dates mainly from 1343 when Edward III granted Robert Bertram a licence to crenellate (or fortify) his mansion house. As at Dunstanburgh, the gatehouse at Bothal was the dominant defensive structure. Strong curtain walls and several towers provided additional protection. Interestingly, in the masonry of the gatehouse battlements are several round holes, which could be quickly opened and closed by hinged shutters. They were designed to give archers greater protection when shooting through the holes. The gatehouse was restored as a house in 1831 and later extended. The castle is not open to the public.

SEATON DELAVAL HALL

Designed by Sir John Vanbrugh for Admiral George Delaval, Seaton Delaval Hall was described as a 'triumph' by Pevsner: 'No other Vanbrugh house is so mature, so compact and so powerful.' Work started on the house in 1718, but by the time it had been completed, some eleven years later, both owner and designer had died. All that remains of the earlier fortified home of the Delavals is their private chapel (now the parish church of Delaval). Standing on a separate site to the Hall, it dates from the end of the eleventh century. Many of the Delavals were buried in the chapel, including Admiral George Delaval (d.1723) and his heir and nephew, Captain Francis Blake Delaval (d.1752). It was during their lifetime, according to Howitt's *Visits to Remarkable Places* (1890), that the Delavals 'acquired a reputation for courtly splendour, profuse living, and open-house jollity'. A fire in 1822 left the Hall a partial ruin. Today the privately owned property, including the magnificent stables and extensive grounds, are regularly open to the public.

ST MARY'S ISLAND, WHITLEY BAY

Situated at the northern end of Whitley Bay, St Mary's Island is connected to the mainland at Curry's Point by a short causeway, covered by the sea at high tide. During medieval times, the monks of Tynemouth Priory maintained a chapel (dedicated to St Helen) and a cemetery on the rocky island. According to tradition, the monks always burned a light in the chapel to warn passing ships of the dangerous rocks nearby. Such lights were known as St Mary's lights, hence the name of the island. In addition to the bodies of monks and drowned sailors, the cemetery also contained the corpses of cholera victims quarantined on the island in 1799. The present lighthouse, thirty-eight metres (126 feet) high, was completed in 1898. It ceased operation in 1984 and, together with the keepers' cottages, now houses a visitor centre. The red-roofed building facing Curry's Point dates from 1855, when George Ewen, a salmon fisherman from Aberdeen, was first given permission to erect a croft on the island. Curry's Point is named after Michael Curry who was hanged there for murder in 1739.

KIELDER WATER

Kielder Water – located within the largest forest in Britain, covering around 125,000 acres – is the largest reservoir in Britain, with a capacity of 200,024 million litres (44,000 million gallons), a surface area of 2,684 acres and a shoreline of over forty-three kms (twenty-seven miles). Its length is over eleven kms (seven miles), making it England's second largest lake; the largest is Lake Windermere. The construction of the dam – 1,143-metres (1,250 yards) long, 387 metres (423 yards) wide and fifty-two-metres (170 feet) high – was completed in 1980, but took a year and a half to fill up. A smaller dam, built further up the valley, forms the Bakethin Reservoir (now designated a nature conservation area). Water from the Kielder reservoir is used to regulate the River Tyne, as well as feed the Wear and the Tees. The flexibility of the system makes water from Kielder available to the major urban areas of north-east England, notably Newcastle and industrial Teesside. Kielder also generates electricity by means of two turbines installed at the dam. As a popular centre for leisure and recreation, Kielder offers a wide range of attractions.

MONUMENT, PADON HILL

Its 1,240-foot (378-metre) high summit crowned with a distinctive 'pepperpot' monument, Padon Hill was named after Alexander Pedon – a Scottish Presbyterian, who held unauthorized religious services on the site during the reign of Charles II, when nonconformists were frequently persecuted. Tradition says that worshippers were expected to show their defiance by adding a stone to the mounting pile at the top of the hill. The present monument was erected in the 1920s and stands some five metres (fifteen feet) high. Passing to the west of the summit is the Pennine Way, the long-distance footpath that stretches 435 kms (270 miles) along the backbone of England – from the Derbyshire village of Edale in the Peak District to the Scottish village of Kirk Yetholm in the Borders. The route was officially opened in 1965. East of Padon Hill, in Redesdale, is Percy's Cross, marking the favoured location for the battle of Otterburn (celebrated in the ballad of *Chevy Chase*). Standing near the site of an earlier 'Battle Stone', the shaft of the cross is a stone lintel from a kitchen fireplace.

BLACK MIDDENS BASTLE HOUSE

Just inside the eastern boundary of the Northumberland National Park, ten kms (six miles) north-west of Bellingham, Black Middens Bastle is a good example of a defensible house built by more prosperous farmers in the sixteenth century to protect themselves and their livestock against attacks from hostile neighbours or raiders from further afield. Before the addition of stone steps, access to the door on the first floor was by means of a removable ladder. This upper floor provided the living accommodation, whilst the lower floor housed cattle or other livestock. The majority of bastles in Northumbria are concentrated in a thirty-two-km (twenty-mile) wide corridor, running along the length of the Anglo-Scottish border. In the late sixteenth and early seventeenth centuries, before the two countries were united under a single crown and relative peace was established, life in this area was lawless and dangerous. For greater protection, therefore, some bastles were built in clusters so help could be close at hand. The remains of Black Middens are now in the care of English Heritage.

CATCLEUGH RESERVOIR, REDESDALE

From its source on the heights of the Cheviot Hills, the River Rede flows south-eastward through Catcleugh Reservoir and Redesdale Forest to join the River North Tyne at Redesmouth, near Bellingham. The reservoir was built between 1890 and 1905 to supply water to Newcastle and Gateshead. Indeed, as the workforce came mostly from these rival towns, they and their families were divided into two camps, known as 'Newcastle' and 'Gateshead'. Wisely, their temporary settlements were situated on opposite sides of the river. Over sixty of those who died during the construction of the reservoir are commemorated in a stained-glass window in the little eighteenth-century church of St Francis of Assisi, one kilometre (half a mile) east of the forestry village of Byrness. A brass plaque beside the window bears their names. According to Tomlinson's *Comprehensive Guide to Northumberland* (1888), Chattlehope farmhouse (shown in the photograph) 'bears the date 1704, and is one of the oldest buildings in the district'. 'Whitelee', further up Redesdale, was once a coaching inn.

BOUGHTHILL, TARSET BURN VALLEY

Before the establishment of law and order in the frontier zones, or Marches, between England and Scotland, the Border people lived in a state of almost continual warfare. In addition to the great battles fought between the English and the Scots, there were frequent skirmishes between the Borderers themselves. The armed gangs of raiders which terrorized the area, attacking farmsteads, killing the inhabitants and stealing their livestock (mainly cattle and horses), were known as reivers. Indeed, so notorious was the reputation of the men of Redesdale and North Tynedale for lawlessness that, until the year 1771, there was a bye-law in Newcastle forbidding employers to take on apprentices born in either of the two valleys. Forays were planned with military precision, the size of the target determining the strength of the raiding party (numbers ranged from less than ten to more than three thousand men). This photograph was taken in the valley of the Tarset Burn, a tributary of the North Tyne and an area in which fortified dwellings were essential.

CHEVIOT HILLS, FROM CARTER BAR

At 1,371 feet (418 metres) above sea-level, Carter Bar stands not only on the boundary between England and Scotland, but also on the watershed between Catcleugh Shin and Arks Edge; with the waters of the River Rede flowing south-eastward into England, and those of the Jed Water flowing northward into Scotland. The word 'Bar' serves as a reminder that a tollhouse stood at the top of the pass in the eighteenth and nineteenth centuries. Carter Bar was known in ancient times as the 'Redeswire' ('swire' meaning a neck of high land). In 1575, it was the scene of a Border conflict between Sir John Forster, the English Warden of the Middle March, and Sir John Carmichael, the Scottish Keeper of Liddesdale. The skirmish is commemorated in the ballad *The Raid of Redeswire*. Apparently, a peaceful meeting between the two men and their followers, developed into a fight which the Scots won. Although Forster and some of his men were taken prisoner, they were eventually released to prevent a war developing between the two nations.

WALLED GARDEN, WALLINGTON

Some five kms (three miles) east of Kirkwhelpington, the National Trust property of Wallington was once the site of a castle (or fortified dwelling) owned by the Fenwicks. In 1688 the estate was purchased by Sir William Blackett, who immediately replaced the Fenwicks' ancestral home with the present courtyard house (remodelled in around 1738 by the architect, Daniel Garrett). The Clock Tower – a stable and coach house topped by a cupola on nine Doric columns – was completed in 1754. Sir Walter Calverley Blackett, who inherited Wallington in 1727, created the gardens and landscaped the park. Fittingly, Lancelot 'Capability' Brown, who was born nearby at Kirkharle in 1715, had a hand in some of the design. The four stone griffin heads on the East Lawn once stood on Bishop's Gate in London. The present appearance of the Walled Garden, originally created as a kitchen garden in about 1765, is mainly due to the Trevelyans, who owned the estate from 1777 to 1941 and who commissioned the famous murals of Northumbrian history inside the house.

PERCY'S CROSS, OTTERBURN

Not only is the exact date of the battle of Otterburn disputed by historians, so is the exact location of the site. The favoured dates are either the 5th, 10th or 19th of August 1388, whilst alternative locations include Greenchesters (near Percy's Cross), Battle Hill (near Elsdon) and Fawdon Hill (north of Otterburn). On Ordnance Survey maps the battlesite is marked near Percy's Cross. What is certain, however, is that somewhere in the locality, in August 1388, the Scots under James, 2nd Earl of Douglas, defeated the English force commanded by Sir Henry Percy (nicknamed 'Hotspur' because of his hot-headed nature). James, however, was killed. Apparently, after ravaging the countryside as far south as Durham, the seven thousand-strong Scots army had captured Hotspur's pennant in a skirmish outside the walls of Newcastle-upon-Tyne. Percy immediately gave chase, without waiting for reinforcements. The subsequent battle – which according to Froissart was 'the hardest and most obstinate battle that ever was fought' – took place at night under a Lammastide moon.

BELSAY CASTLE

Apart from a short break in the late fourteenth century, Belsay Castle was the principal seat of the Middleton family for over five hundred years. The earliest part of the present structure is the fourteenth-century tower house, which was extended by the addition of an unfortified manor house in the early seventeenth century. Little remains of the large west wing, built in 1711. The family moved out of the castle and into their new home, Belsay Hall, on Christmas Day 1817. During Victorian times the castle was remodelled as a steward's residence. Belsay Hall was designed in neo-Greek style by Sir Charles Monck (formerly Middleton). He also extended the park and demolished the village of Belsay, rebuilding it a kilometre to the east. The quarry that provided the stone for building the Hall was turned into a series of unusual gardens, also designed by Monck. Today they are considered to be the property's finest feature. Although the park and estate still belong to the Middletons, Belsay Hall, Castle and Gardens are in the care of English Heritage.

PARISH CHURCH, ELSDON

The parish church of St Cuthbert in the village of Elsdon, some five kms (three miles) east of Otterburn, was built around 1400 on the site of an earlier, Norman foundation. Towards the end of the eleventh century, Robert de Umfraville (Robert-with-the-Beard) erected a motte-and-bailey castle nearby to defend his lands in neighbouring Redesdale. The Umfravilles' key fortification nearest the Anglo-Scottish border, it was eventually superseded by Harbottle Castle in Coquetdale. It is thought that the rebuilding of the church and the erection of the Vicar's Pele (fortified parsonage) may have followed a particularly devastating raid by the Scots around the close of the fourteenth century. Many of those killed at the battle of Otterburn in 1388 were buried in Elsdon churchyard. Among the numerous stones of interest in the church is an inscribed Roman tombstone from nearby *Bremenium* (Rochester). The deep grooves in the pillar near the entrance are said to have been made by Elsdon men sharpening their weapons before leaving the church.

WINTER'S GIBBET, NEAR ELSDON

In 1791 – at Steng Cross, near Battle Hill, some three kms (two miles) south-east of Elsdon – the body of William Winter was hung in chains from a gibbet, within sight of the place where he had murdered old Margaret Crozier. The present gibbet, with a wooden head suspended from it, was erected on the exact site of the original and is mentioned in Tomlinson's *Comprehensive Guide to Northumberland* (1888). Apparently, Winter – 'a desperate character, but recently returned from transportation' – went to his victim's house at 'Haws Pele', Raw, five kms (three miles) north of Elsdon, at the instigation of Jane and Eleanor Clark. These two women, 'vendors of crockery and tinwork', had previously visited the pele and noted that it was worth robbing. All three took part in the crime. They were captured and convicted on evidence given by a shepherd boy, who had seen them resting and eating in a sheepfold, and 'taken particular notice of the number and character of the nails in Winter's shoes, and also the peculiar gulley or butcher's knife with which he divided the food'.

HEXHAM ABBEY

Occupying high ground on the south side of the River Tyne, the ancient market town of Hexham grew up beside the monastery founded in about 674 by St Wilfrid. Shortly after, the church – dedicated to St Andrew the Apostle – became a cathedral. Tunberht (or Trumbrith), the first bishop of the new see of Hexham, was consecrated in 681. From the late eighth century Northumbria suffered from increasingly severe Danish raids and, in 875, the abbey at Hexham was plundered and destroyed. It was refounded as a priory of Augustinian canons by Thomas II, Archbishop of York, in 1113. There followed a century of relative peace and prosperity, during which time the canons acquired the relics of at least six saints. In 1296, the Scots sacked and burned the town. The priory was gutted by fire and all its priceless treasures, including the saintly shrines, were either stolen or destroyed. Further raids followed, notably in 1297 and in 1346. In 1537 the priory was dissolved. Its church was extensively restored in Victorian and Edwardian times.

BLANCHLAND

Located in the upper Derwent Valley, some fourteen kms (nine miles) south of Hexham, Blanchland is an attractive stone village of mainly eighteenth- and early nineteenth-century houses, built around a large L-shaped square. Its origins date back to the twelfth century, when monks of the Premonstratensian Order established a monastery on the site. Blanchland, meaning 'white land', is thought to have been named after the white habit worn by the canons. After the dissolution of the monasteries, the abbey first belonged to the Radcliffes and then, in about 1623, to the Forsters of Bamburgh. The Blanchland and Bamburgh estates were purchased by Nathaniel, Lord Crewe, Bishop of Durham in 1704 and, on his death in 1721, they were bequeathed to a charitable trust. The Lord Crewe Trustees were responsible for rebuilding Blanchland village and the abbey church (parts of the latter were incorporated into the eighteenth-century parish church). Substantial evidence of the medieval monastery can still be found throughout the village today.

GEORGE STEPHENSON'S BIRTHPLACE, WYLAM

Born in High Street House, Wylam, on 9 June 1781, George Stephenson – the world-famous railway engineer – was the son of a pit pumping-engine fireman at Wylam Colliery. At the time, the house (now owned by the National Trust) was divided into tenements for four miners' families. The Stephensons – George, his mother and father, plus the rest of the brood – all occupied a small, cramped single room on the ground floor. They only moved when George was eight. The walls were without plaster, the ceiling had exposed rafters and the floor was beaten earth. Running past the house was the wooden-railed wagonway, along which coal was transported from the colliery to the River Tyne at Lemington, eight kms (five miles) to the east. The wagons were horse-drawn. At around the age of ten, George started work at the colliery alongside his father. He learned fast, including how to read and write, and eventually, after leaving Wylam, began to design his own steam locomotives. The company formed by George and his son, Robert, built the 'Locomotion' (1825) and the 'Rocket' (1830).

PARISH CHURCH, HEAVENFIELD

The parish church of St Oswald in Lee – standing alone on a hill overlooking Hadrian's Wall, some five kms (three miles) north of Hexham – was rebuilt in 1737 on the site of at least two earlier foundations. According to tradition, the first church was built to commemorate the battle of Heavenfield (634), in which Cadwaladr (Cadwalla or Cadwallon), King of Gwynedd, was defeated and killed by Oswald (son of Ethelfrith, King of Northumbria) who was converted to Christianity on Iona. Immediately after the battle, Oswald was accepted as King of Northumbria, thereby reuniting the two Anglo-Saxon kingdoms of Deira (with a capital at York) and Bernicia (with a capital at Bamburgh). Victory, so it was believed, had been achieved with the assistance of God for, prior to the battle, Oswald had knelt and prayed before a wooden cross specifically erected for the purpose. The site became a place of pilgrimage. In 642, after he had been slain at the battle of Maserfield (Oswestry) by Penda, King of Mercia, Oswald was venerated as a saint and martyr.

PRUDHOE CASTLE

Strategically sited on a steep-sided spur, overlooking an ancient crossing of the River Tyne and on the route from Newcastle to Carlisle, Prudhoe Castle is thought to date from the late eleventh century, when the Norman knight, Robert-with-the-Beard, was granted Prudhoe and lands in Redesdale by either William the Conqueror or William Rufus. His descendant, Robert de Umfraville, was formally granted the barony of Prudhoe by Henry I, together with permission to build a castle. The original earth and timber fortress was probably replaced by a stronger and more permanent structure of stone during the mid- to late twelfth century. The gatehouse and keep, however, may be earlier. In 1173, and again in 1174, the fortress was besieged by William the Lion, King of Scotland. Despite having close links with the Scottish court, Odinel de Umfraville II took part in William's capture at Alnwick. The remains of Prudhoe Castle, including the Georgian Manor House built by the 2nd Duke of Northumberland, are now in the care of English Heritage.

TOWN & ROMAN FORT, CORBRIDGE

The Roman fort at Corbridge (the name of which is not known with certainty, but may have been something like *Corstopitum* or *Coriosopitum*) was strategically positioned on a terrace to guard the point where the north–south Dere Street crossed the River Tyne. It also marked the beginning of the Stanegate route to Carlisle. Excavations have revealed that there was an earlier settlement on the site. The first Roman fort in the locality was erected about a kilometre to the west (near Red House farm) in about AD 79. It was abandoned some five years later in favour of the first of at least four other forts on the *Corstopitum* site. By the early third century, the military fort had developed into a flourishing garrison town and supply base for troops on Hadrian's Wall. Its remains are now in the care of English Heritage. Less than a kilometre to the east lies the old market town and former borough of Corbridge, founded in Anglo-Saxon times. Many Roman stones were used in the construction of the buildings, including the parish church of St Andrew and the nearby Vicar's Pele.

AYDON CASTLE, NEAR CORBRIDGE

Originally built as a manor house in the last quarter of the thirteenth century by a wealthy Suffolk merchant, Robert de Reymes, Aydon Castle (or Hall) was fortified in 1305 after the resumption of hostilities between England and Scotland. Robert took part in numerous campaigns against William Wallace and the Scots, including the battles of Stirling Bridge (1297) and Falkirk (1298). For several years he also served under Robert de Umfraville, Earl of Angus, who was captured at Bannockburn in 1314 and deprived of his Scottish title and estates. In the spring of 1315, Robert left Aydon Castle, well stocked with provisions, in the custody of Hugh de Gales. At the approach of a Scottish army, de Gales immediately surrendered. The house was subsequently sacked and burned. Two years later, to rub salt into the wound, the building suffered further damage at the hands of de Gales and a party of English rebels. The castle, converted into a farmhouse in the seventeenth century, is now in the care of English Heritage.

BERWICK-UPON-TWEED & THE
NORTH-EASTERN BORDER

ðŧ

OLD BRIDGE, BERWICK-UPON-TWEED

Ownership of the ancient Border town of Berwick – at the mouth of the Tweed – is said to have alternated between England and Scotland no less than fourteen times during the thirteenth to fifteenth centuries. It finally became English territory in 1482, when the Scots surrendered the town to Richard, Duke of Gloucester (later Richard III). Even then, it continued to suffer repeated hostilities until the two countries were united under one crown in 1603. Tradition says that the Old Bridge (or Berwick Bridge) was built on the orders of James VI of Scotland. Apparently, whilst crossing the previous bridge on his journey south to become James I of England, he condemned the wooden structure as unsafe. Built of red sandstone, the fifteen-arch Old Bridge was completed in 1634 and is 355 metres (1,164 feet) long. The New Bridge (or Royal Tweed Bridge) nearby was erected in the late 1920s. Further upstream, the twenty-eight-arch Royal Border Bridge, dating from 1850, was designed by Robert Stephenson to carry the London–Edinburgh railway above the river.

Celtic Christianity existed in Britain during Roman times, long before Pope Gregory the Great sent his missionary, St Augustine, to England in 597 to try and convert the Anglo-Saxons to the religion of Rome. It seems that the earliest Britons to adopt the Christian faith, did so in the second and third centuries, when followers of the 'cult of Jesus Christ' were cruelly persecuted by the Romans. The province's first Christian martyr was St Alban (Albanus), a pagan soldier from the city of *Verulamium* (St Albans). In 208 (the earliest of several possible dates) he sheltered a priest from the authorities and was converted by him to Christianity. When soldiers surrounded the house, Albanus put on the robes of the priest and was arrested, tortured and finally executed in his stead. Among the miraculous signs that accompanied the saint's death was the immediate conversion of his first executioner, who promptly refused to carry out the beheading. His replacement, however, had no such qualms. But, as soon as he had dealt the fatal blow, his eyes dramatically fell out of their sockets. The martyrdom of St Alban, together with the story of the conversion of the pagan Anglo-Saxons to Christianity, was chronicled in *The Ecclesiastical History of the English People* by the Venerable Bede (673–735), a Benedictine monk of the dual monastery of St Peter and St Paul at Wearmouth (Monkwearmouth) and Jarrow.

At the end of this influential and celebrated work, Bede recorded a brief note about himself:

I was born in the territory of this monastery, and, on reaching the age of seven, my family entrusted my education, first to the reverend Abbot Benedict [Biscop of Wearmouth] and then to Abbot Ceolfrith [of Jarrow]. Since that time, I have spent my whole life in this monastery, devoting myself entirely to the study of the scriptures. And, whilst I have observed the regular discipline and the daily obligation of singing in church, my principal delight has always been in learning, teaching and writing.

Bede lived during the period which is, somewhat paradoxically, known as both the 'Dark Ages' and the 'Golden Age of Anglo-Saxon Northumbria'. His ecclesiastical history reflects the prevailing belief and culture of the age – almost one thousand years before the dawn of scientific enlightenment. Understandably, therefore, his history places as much importance on the miraculous as it does on the more mundane.

The early history of Christianity in Northumbria is essentially the story of two lengthy conflicts: the struggle against paganism and idolatry; and the divergence, within the religion itself, between the Roman and the more austere Celtic Church. The latter was finally resolved at the Synod of Whitby in 664, when it was decided that the authority of Rome should be adopted in preference to that of the Celtic Christian Church in Britain.

Although Christianity was eventually embraced by the Romans, especially by those who lived in the frontier towns and forts along Hadrian's Wall, it was virtually extinguished in the province after the departure of the legions in the early fifth century. It was replaced by the worship of pagan deities introduced by Germanic settlers and invaders from northern Europe (Angles, Saxons, Jutes and others). Nevertheless, the culture, religion and traditions of the native Britons, or Celts, survived in the northern and western extremities of the British Isles, where the mountainous terrain (or the sea in the case of Ireland) proved too formidable an obstacle for conquest.

The reintroduction of Celtic Christianity into pagan Northumbria came from the Scottish island of Iona, off the south-west tip of Mull in the Inner Hebrides. Although it provided a safe haven for Druids, or Celtic priests, fleeing from persecution by the conquering Romans, the first Christian monastery on the small island was founded by St Columba after his flight from Ireland in 563. The community soon became a major centre of the Celtic Church, sending out missionaries to mainland Scotland and Northumbria, including St Aidan, the founder and first abbot of the monastery at Lindisfarne (Holy Island). The man who invited and encouraged Aidan to cross the Border into northern England was Oswald, second son of Ethelfrith, King of Northumbria.

Ethelfrith – whom Bede called 'a very strong king and most eager for glory' – was originally the ruler of the northern Northumbrian kingdom of Bernicia (with its capital at Bamburgh), but extended his power to include Deira (with its capital at York) by marrying a daughter of Aelle, King of Deira. In 616, after he had been killed in battle by Raedwald, King of the East Angles, Ethelfrith was succeeded by his brother-in-law, Edwin. In consequence, Oswald and his two brothers, Eanfrid and Oswy, were forced into exile among the Picts and Scots. During part of this time they stayed at the monastery of Iona, where all three were converted to Christianity.

According to Bede, Edwin – who married Ethelburga, a Christian princess from Kent – 'ruled over all the inhabitants of Britain, English and Britons alike, and also brought the islands of Anglesey and Man under his power'. He was converted to Roman Christianity by Paulinus, a missionary monk sent by Pope Gregory the Great, who accompanied Ethelburga north on her betrothal in 625. Paulinus, who became the first bishop of York, succeeded in baptizing thousands of Northumbrians. Bede wrote:

> So great was the fervour of the faith and the desire for the cleansing of salvation among the Northumbrians, that when Paulinus visited the king and queen in their royal palace of Adgefrin [Yeavering], he remained thirty-six days there, fully occupied in the task of catechizing and baptising. During which time, from morning till night, he did nothing else but instruct the masses, who flocked to him from every village and district, in the salvation of Christ.

In 633, Edwin was defeated and killed in a battle near Doncaster by the pagan Penda, King of Mercia, and his ally, Cadwaladr, King of Gwynedd. As a result, the Northumbrian kingdom was once more divided. Eanfrid, the eldest son of Ethelfrith, became King of Bernicia and Osric became King of Deira. Paulinus fled with Ethelburga to Kent, and Christianity, which both Eanfrid and Osric renounced to return to the pagan beliefs of most of their subjects, was almost extinguished in Northumbria. The reigns of Eanfrid and Osric were short-lived, however, for within a year both were slain by Cadwaladr, who, according to Bede, 'ruled the territories of Northumbria, not as a victorious king, but as a savage and bloody tyrant'.

Eanfrid's brother, Oswald, decided to try and regain the kingdom from Cadwaladr. The opposing armies met in 634 at Deniseburn (later called Heavenfield) close to Hadrian's Wall, north of Hexham. On the eve of the battle, St Columba appeared in a vision and told Oswald (who unlike his elder brother did not abandon the Christian faith) that if he remained strong and courageous God would deliver Cadwaladr into his hands. Just before the fight, Oswald erected a wooden cross, then he and his followers knelt before it and prayed for heavenly help in defeating Cadwaladr's Celtic army (made up of both pagans and Christians) and liberating the people of Northumbria. According to Bede, they then:

> advanced towards the enemy just as dawn was breaking, and achieved the victory that their faith deserved. In the place where they prayed, countless miracles of healing are known to have been performed, as a token and memorial of the king's faith.

Victory made Oswald the new king of a reunited Northumbria, ruling a territory that stretched south to the Humber and north to the Firth of Forth. He was probably also 'Bretwalda' (overlord) of other Anglo-Saxon kingdoms. Mindful of where he himself had been baptized, Oswald invited the monks of Iona to send a missionary to convert his people to Christianity. They sent St Aidan, who chose to set up a monastery on Lindisfarne, near the royal capital of Bamburgh. It was from this base – this second Iona – that Christian worship in its Celtic form spread and became widely accepted in Northumbria and beyond.

Oswald was killed in 642 at the battle of Maserfield (Oswestry) by Penda. Although his body was sacrificially dismembered, the parts are said to have been recovered and dispersed in different places. His head was buried at Lindisfarne, his hands and arms at Bamburgh, and his body at Bardney in Lincolnshire. Venerated as a saint and martyr, Oswald's various shrines became centres of pilgrimage and the sites of oft-reported miracles. The Cult of St Oswald, which eventually spread to Europe where it was popular throughout the Middle Ages, was encouraged by Oswy, who became King of Northumbria after his brother's death. It was Oswy who presided over the Synod held at Whitby in 664, where the long-standing differences between the Roman and Celtic strands of Christianity were settled in favour of Rome.

Towards the end of the century, Northumbrian power began to wane and, by the middle of the eighth century, Mercia had become the dominant kingdom in England. In 793 the Vikings from Scandinavia crossed the sea in their dragon-ships and raided the monastery at Lindisfarne, murdering many of the monks and carrying off others as slaves. Although the pagan raiders had made small forays along the Northumbrian coast before, the attack on Lindisfarne marked the real beginning of the Viking Age in Britain. Over the next few years, they ventured further afield, plundering – with increasing violence and frequency – the coasts of Ireland, Wales and western Scotland (including the monastery at Iona).

The first Viking to rule over the whole of Anglo-Saxon England was Cnut, or Canute, who was elected king in 1016. Even the Normans, who invaded the island under William the Conqueror in 1066, were the descendants of Vikings. One consequence of linking island Britain with mainland Europe under the Normans was the revitalization of Christianity, especially monasticism. Religious houses were founded or refounded, first for Benedictines, and later for other orders. The Normans also introduced a new warrior breed of Christians into Northumbria: the powerful Prince Bishops of Durham, who ruled a palatinate on the edge of the Anglo-Scottish Border – a turbulent frontier where lawlessness, bloodshed, terrorism and blackmail prevailed until well into the seventeenth century. Whilst the rulers of England and Scotland battled for control of the territory – particularly for the much-coveted frontier town of Berwick-upon-Tweed – the Borderers took to robbing and feuding amongst themselves. No one was immune to the fear engendered by the sound of approaching hoof-beats. The time of the Border reivers – the wild raiders who wore steel bonnets and padded jackets – had come.

JUBILEE COTTAGE, FORD

In 1859, shortly after her husband had been killed in a hunting accident, Louisa, Marchioness of Waterford, remodelled Ford Castle and completely rebuilt the village. The thirteenth-century church of St Michael & All Saints, however, was retained (in fact, it had been restored in 1853 by John Dobson, the Newcastle architect). At the western end of the village's single street, the Marchioness erected a monument to her dead husband – a tall granite pillar surmounted by an angel. At the eastern end, she built a cottage to commemorate the 1887 Golden Jubilee of Queen Victoria. It housed a nurse whose services were free to all living on the estate. Lady Waterford Hall in the village centre was a school from 1860 to 1957. Inside, the Marchioness painted a large series of biblical scenes, using some villagers as models. Ruskin (who had taught her to paint) commented: 'I expected you would have done something better.' The village blacksmith's forge, dating from 1863, has a door surrounded by a massive stone horseshoe.

RAVENSDOWNE BARRACKS, BERWICK-UPON-TWEED

Occupying a strategic position on the once-turbulent frontier between Scotland and England, Berwick-upon-Tweed was fortified on successive occasions. During medieval times, the town – lying on the north side of the river – was protected not only by the castle (first built in the twelfth century and now a ruin), but also encircled by a wall. In the mid-sixteenth century, when Scottish and/or French invasion seemed a strong possibility, it was decided to strengthen the town's defences against an artillery attack with a system of gateways, ramparts and projecting bastions, or platforms. Today, the Elizabethan ramparts are considered the best example of their type in Britain. The Ravensdowne Barracks, begun in 1717, are among the earliest purpose-built barracks in the United Kingdom. They were first occupied by troops in 1721 and became the regimental headquarters of the King's Own (Scottish) Borderers in 1881. The barracks, the ramparts and the castle remains are all now in the care of English Heritage.

ETAL CASTLE

From the mid-twelfth century until 1547, Etal Castle belonged to the Manners family, ancestors of the present Dukes of Rutland. The original manor house that stood on the site was first replaced by a tower house (shown in the photograph). Permission to crenellate, or fortify, the house was granted in 1341. Robert Manners decided to strengthen his home, partly because of Scottish raids and partly because of disputes with his neighbour, William Heron of Ford Castle. Indeed, the rivalry between both families developed into a feud, which reached its climax in 1427, when John Manners killed a later William Heron for leading an attack on Etal. By the time the feud ended in 1439, the castle was in a very dilapidated state. It remained the family residence, however, until around the beginning of the sixteenth century. In 1513 it was seized by King James IV of Scotland and, after his defeat at Flodden, the captured Scottish cannon were stored in the basement of the tower house. The property is now in the care of English Heritage.

NORHAM CASTLE

Standing on the English side of the River Tweed, some sixteen kms (ten miles) upstream of Berwick, the Border castle at Norham was rebuilt in stone with strong walls and a great keep in about 1160 by Hugh de Puiset, Bishop of Durham. It occupies the site of a motte-and-bailey castle, built by Bishop Ranulph Flambard in 1121. Despite withstanding countless sieges and attacks, the stronghold was captured and badly damaged by the invading Scottish army of James IV in 1513. In his long poem *Marmion* (also called *A Tale of Flodden Field*), Sir Walter Scott wrote in 'Canto First':

Day set on Norham's castled steep,
And Tweed's fair river, broad and
   deep,
And Cheviot's mountains lone:
The battled towers, the donjon
   keep,
The loophole grates, where captives
   weep,
The flanking walls that round it
   sweep,
In yellow lustre shone.

The remains of the castle (the most substantial parts of which date from the fifteenth and sixteenth centuries) are now in the care of English Heritage. J. M. W. Turner depicted the ruins in several of his paintings.

RIVER TWEED, CORNHILL-ON-TWEED

Rising on the Scottish hills south of Edinburgh, the River Tweed flows eastward for some 156 kms (ninety-seven miles) to enter the North Sea at Berwick-upon-Tweed in England. For the twenty-seven-km (seventeen-mile) stretch from Berwick to Kelso (but excluding both towns) the river forms the border between the two countries. Among the English towns and villages along the Tweed border are Carham, Cornhill, Norham and Horncliffe. A short distance downstream from the latter, the river is crossed by the Union Chain Bridge, built in 1820 by Samuel Brown, and the first suspension bridge in Britain to use wrought-iron chains. Brown's links (which he patented) were used by Thomas Telford in 1826 for the 386-metre (1,265-foot) long Menai Strait Bridge in North Wales. The earliest suspension bridge to have been built in Britain is said to have been the Wynch Bridge in Teesdale, erected by lead miners in the early eighteenth century, but replaced in 1830. The only tributary of the Tweed to lie entirely in England is the River Till. Their confluence is a few miles downstream of Cornhill.

COLDSTREAM BRIDGE

Spanning both the River Tweed and the Anglo-Scottish border at Coldstream, this elegant seven-arch bridge was constructed in the 1760s by John Smeaton, a civil engineer and architect, who not only built bridges at Perth and Banff in Scotland, but also the 1759 Eddystone lighthouse in the English Channel (re-erected in 1884 on Plymouth Hoe). The bridge he designed over the Tyne at Hexham was destroyed by a flood in 1782. Like the smithy at Gretna Green, the tollhouse on the Scottish side of the Coldstream bridge was once a popular marriage destination for runaway couples. A bronze plaque attached to the bridge in 1926 commemorates Robert Burns' crossing of 7 May 1787, when he entered England for the first time. Kneeling, the Scottish poet prayed for a blessing on his native land with the words:

O Scotia! my dear, my native soil!
For whom my warmest wish to
    Heaven is sent!
Long may thy hardy sons of rustic
    toil
Be blest with health, and peace, and
    sweet content.

On the English side of the bridge is the village of Cornhill-on-Tweed.

FLODDEN BATTLEFIELD, NEAR BRANXTON

On Piper's Hill, south-west of the church of St Paul at Branxton, is a tall granite cross, unveiled in 1910 to commemorate the Battle of Flodden, fought on 9 September 1513. During the first two years of the reign of Henry VIII relations between England and Scotland were friendly. Nevertheless, in 1512 James IV of Scotland decided to renew the 'Auld Alliance' with France, in which both countries promised mutual support should either be attacked by England – the 'auld enemy'. Inevitably, when Henry invaded France in the summer of 1513, James invaded Northumbria, capturing the castles at Norham and Ford. The English army, led by Thomas Howard, Earl of Surrey, marched north and found the Scots camped in a virtually impregnable position on Flodden Hill, three kms (two miles) south-east of Branxton. During the battle, James abandoned the high ground to fall upon the enemy. Defeat quickly followed. Estimates as to the number of Scotsmen killed range from five to ten thousand, including some two dozen noblemen and the King of Scotland himself.

PARISH CHURCH, ANCROFT

Eight kms (five miles) south of Berwick-upon-Tweed, the parish church of St Anne at Ancroft dates from Norman times, when it was a mainland chapelry of the monks of Lindisfarne Priory. The fortified three-storey pele tower was added to the western end of the nave and chancel in the late thirteenth or early fourteenth century. By the early nineteenth century the building was so dilapidated that a large ash tree grew in the middle of the tower, 'supported on an arch, where its roots are sustained by the decaying of the walls' (quoted in the church guide). Subsequent restoration included the destruction of the Norman chancel, the building of a new chancel and the extension of the nave to the east. Near the tower is a headstone, marking the grave of ten nuns who fled to England during the French Revolution (1789–99) and were given sanctuary at nearby Haggerston Castle. The original village of Ancroft stood in the field south-west of the church. It was abandoned after most of the inhabitants fell victim to the plague in 1667.

CUP-AND-RING MARKED ROCK, ROUGHTING LINN

Scattered throughout Northumbria, especially on remote hillsides, rocks can be found decorated with mysterious cup-and-ring markings, and occasionally spirals. The largest inscribed rock in the region stands near the Iron Age hillfort of Roughting Linn, five kms (three miles) east of Ford. Around eighteen metres (sixty feet) long, twelve metres (forty feet) wide and three metres (ten feet) high, the sandstone rock is covered with carvings that not only include hollow 'cups' surrounded by rings, but grooves, rectangles and motifs that look like stars, plants and flowers. The purpose and exact date of the symbols, however, remains obscure. Although widely attributed to the Bronze Age, their origins may lie further back in the Neolithic period, around five thousand years ago. Their significance is often said to be religious or ceremonial, but they could equally be maps, games or even prehistoric doodles. Tomlinson, in his *Comprehensive Guide to Northumberland* (1888), suggested that 'they may have been connected with the obscene Phallic worship once so prevalent among primitive peoples.'

BOATSHEDS, LINDISFARNE

In the vicinity of Lindisfarne harbour are a number of upturned boats that have been cut in half and converted into storehouses. The three in the photograph – placed near the steep ramp leading to Lindisfarne Castle by Edwin Lutyens in the early twentieth century – were used to store fuel and firewood. All serve as a reminder that the island once supported a flourishing herring-fishing industry. In 1859, at the height of its prosperity, Walter White wrote in *Northumberland & the Border*: 'We passed the beach where the fishing-boats come in, and saw the huge wooden vat – if vat it be – round which the women stand to clean the herrings, and on the other side of the road fourteen hundred herring-barrels in piles and rows, and two men industrious over their final preparation. "There wouldn't be any too many", they said, "nor yet half enough, if the boats did but have luck".' Not far from the castle are the remains of lime kilns, dating from the mid-nineteenth century. By 1900, the herring-fishing and lime industries on Lindisfarne had ceased to exist.

LINDISFARNE CASTLE

Using stone from the dissolved priory, Lindisfarne Castle was built in about the middle of the sixteenth century to defend the harbour against Scottish raids. Although the Tudor fort lost much of its importance after England and Scotland were united under one king, James I, a garrison remained until the middle of the nineteenth century. In 1635 Sir William Brereton recorded that the governor of the fort, Captain Rugg, 'is as famous for his generous and free entertainment of strangers as for his great bottle nose, which is the largest I have seen'. Strengthened during the Civil War, the garrison was reduced to seven men by 1715. In that same year the two men on duty were tricked into letting two Jacobite supporters capture the fort, albeit for only one night. In 1903 Edwin Lutyens converted the castle into a country residence for Edward Hudson, the founder of *Country Life* magazine. The small walled garden to the north was designed by Gertrude Jekyll in about 1911. Both garden and castle were acquired by the National Trust in 1944.

LINDISFARNE PRIORY

The Holy Island of Lindisfarne –
once one of the most important
centres of Celtic Christianity in
England – is linked to the mainland
by a causeway one-and-a-half kms
(one mile) long, passable only at
low tide. The island's first monastery
was founded by St Aidan, an Irish
monk of Iona who was invited to
preach in Northumbria shortly after
the convert, Oswald, became king
in 634. Although Aidan was the first
of the Holy Island bishops, the
greatest and most famous was St
Cuthbert, who died on the Inner
Farne in 687 and was buried in St
Peter's church on Lindisfarne.
Eleven years later, his grave was
opened and, according to Bede, the
body was found to be incorrupt,
'more like one asleep than a dead
person'. Hostile incursions by the
Vikings forced the monks to
abandon Lindisfarne in 875, taking
with them the precious relics of
Cuthbert and the beautifully
illuminated Lindisfarne Gospels.
The priory, founded by Benedictine
monks from Durham in the late
eleventh century, was dissolved in
1537. Today the ruins are in the
care of English Heritage.

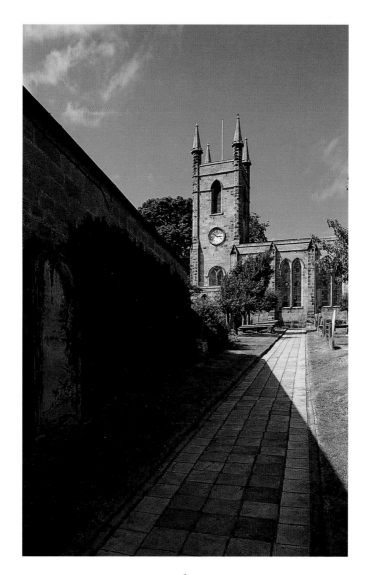

PARISH CHURCH, BELFORD

The parish church of St Mary at
Belford, eight kms (five miles) west
of Bamburgh, was almost entirely
rebuilt in 1828–9 by John Dobson
(1787–1865), whom Pevsner
considered to be 'among the best
architects of his generation in the
whole of England'. (He also
remodelled the eighteenth-century
Belford Hall by James Paine.)
Although the Norman chancel arch
of the church was probably part of
the original twelfth-century
building, some claim that it came
from a small chapel that once stood
to the north of the village. Marking
the seventeenth-century rebuilding
of St Mary's is the date 1615, carved
over a doorway. The clock, which
was installed in the tower in 1841, is
unusual in that it has three rather
than four marks between each five
minutes. In 1966 the vault under
the vestry was discovered. It
contained several lead coffins
belonging to the Atkinson-Clark
family, who lived at Belford Hall
until 1923. In the churchyard is the
grave of Thomas Purdy, who
helped Dorothy Forster of
Bamburgh rescue her brother,
General Tom Forster, from
Newgate prison in 1716.

BUDLE BAY, FROM BUDLE POINT

Almost enclosed by a spit of firm sand, Budle Bay – north of Bamburgh – is a flat and treacherous expanse of estuarine mud and clay. Once an important harbour, it is now a nature reserve inhabited only by seabirds and wildfowl. The deep and narrow channel at the mouth of the bay is formed by the waters of Elwick Burn and Waren Burn. The eighteenth-century mill in the hamlet of Waren Mill stands on the site of several grain mills, the earliest dating from at least 1187. During the thirteenth century, Henry III founded the port and borough of Warenmouth (or Warnmouth), on the southern shore of Budle Bay. The settlement (later called Newtown), together with its harbour, declined after 1482 when Berwick-upon-Tweed became permanent English territory. Today, the port no longer exists. About one-and-a-half kms (one mile) south of Waren Mill is Spindlestone Heugh, the hill associated with the legend of the Laidley (or loathsome) Worm, which terrorized the neighbour-hood of Bamburgh and Budle Bay. It is one of several Northumbrian 'worm' legends.

GRACE DARLING'S TOMB, BAMBURGH

Bamburgh is noted for being the birthplace of Grace Darling (1815–42), who became a national heroine in 1838 after braving tumultuous seas in a small rowing boat with her father to rescue survivors of the stricken steamer *Forfarshire*. At the time she was living on the Farne Island of Longstone, where her father, William Darling, was the lighthouse keeper. According to his journal, the *Forfarshire* set sail from Hull at midnight on 6 September bound for Dundee with a cargo of 'superfine cloths, hardware, soap, boiler plate and spinning-gear'. Early on the morning of 7 September, during a gale, the steamer struck the west point of Big Harcar and most of the passengers were drowned. From her bedroom window, Grace spotted the wreck and, together with her father, managed to rescue eight men and one woman who were desperately clinging to a rock. Grace died of consumption at the age of twenty-six and was buried in Bamburgh churchyard. The boat used in the rescue is preserved in the Grace Darling Museum nearby.

LONGSTONE LIGHTHOUSE, FARNE ISLANDS

Famous for its association with Grace Darling, the lighthouse on Longstone was built in 1826 to replace the 1810 lighthouse on Brownsman. The latter was sited too close to the mainland to prevent ships from being wrecked on the outer islands, especially Knivestone, seven kms (four-and-a-half miles) from the shore. Like the Inner Farne lighthouse, the Longstone lighthouse was designed by David Alexander for Trinity House. It was subsequently enlarged by Joseph Nelson. Nearly half of the almost thirty Farne Islands, which form the most easterly outcrop of the Great Whin Sill, are submerged at high tide. In 1925 the islands were acquired by the National Trust. Today they are an important nature reserve and bird sanctuary. In addition to supporting a large colony of grey seals, the islands are the breeding-ground of seabirds like puffins, eider duck, fulmar, arctic tern, kittiwakes and guillemots. Boat trips around the islands are organized from the fishing port of Seahouses, five kms (three miles) south-east of Bamburgh.

INNER FARNE, FARNE ISLANDS

Revealing an area of some sixteen acres at low water, the Inner Farne is the largest of the Farne Islands. Lying only two and a half kms (a mile-and-a-half) from the mainland, it is famous for being the favoured island of St Cuthbert, and the place where he died in 687. Before the saint retired to live in solitude on the Inner Farne, it is said that he had to banish the demons that haunted it to a nearby rock. These creatures were described as being little black-complexioned men in cowls, who rode goats and brandished lances. Bede records that it was whilst meditating on Inner Farne in 642 that St Aidan (who preceded Cuthbert as Bishop of Lindisfarne) saw the Mercian army under the pagan king Penda attacking Bamburgh. His prayers were said to change the direction of the wind, blowing the flames away from the royal city and into the faces of the heathens. Today, the island's most conspicuous feature is the white 1809 lighthouse. A stone pele tower, built by Thomas Castell, Prior of Durham, in about 1500, stands near the fourteenth-century St Cuthbert's chapel.

BAMBURGH CASTLE

The first fortress on the Great Whin Sill outcrop at Bamburgh, according to the *Anglo-Saxon Chronicle*, was erected in 547 by Ida, King of Bernicia (the northern half of the Anglo-Saxon kingdom of Northumbria). When Ida's grandson, Ethelfrith, King of Northumbria from 593 to 616, gave the fortress to his first wife, Bebba, the settlement became known as 'Bebba's Burgh' or 'Bebbanburgh' (from which the name Bamburgh is derived). After the Norman Conquest, the castle was rebuilt in stone as a Border fortress against incursions by the Scots. It became the first castle in England to fall to artillery fire, when it was captured by Edward IV during the Wars of the Roses. In 1610 the Crown gave the property to Claudius Forster, whose descendants allowed the castle to fall into decay. Restoration of the castle was begun in the eighteenth century by Nathaniel Crewe, Bishop of Durham, and completed at great expense by the Victorian industrialist (and owner of Cragside), William, 1st Lord Armstrong, whose family still owns the property. It is open to the public.

LORDENSHAWS HILLFORT, ROTHBURY HILLS

Situated on high moorland, south of Rothbury and almost 880 feet (268 metres) above sea-level, the Iron Age hillfort at Lordenshaws is thought to date from around 350 BC. Comprising a central area encircled by a series of defensive banks and ditches, the earthwork has two entrances (one to the east and another to the west), both of which are approached by a sunken trackway. Within part of the central area can be found traces of a small settlement of round stone huts, probably dating from later Romano-British times. On the surrounding moorland are several rock outcrops with grooves and cup-and-ring markings, the meaning and purpose of which remain a mystery. The numerous cairns (small mounds of stones) which litter the area south of the fort are thought to have been made by farmers clearing stones from the land before ploughing. The cairns to the north-east, however, are Bronze Age burial mounds. Running north–south, to the west of the fort, are the remains of the boundary wall of the medieval deer park.

CRAGSIDE, NEAR ROTHBURY

Set in over one thousand acres of wooded pleasure grounds, one-and-a-half kms (one mile) east of Rothbury, the Victorian mansion of Cragside was mainly designed by Richard Norman Shaw for William, 1st Lord Armstrong, a wealthy inventor, engineer and gunmaker. Under Armstrong's direction, Shaw transformed the original house, built between 1863 and 1866, into a magnificent country mansion with a mixture of styles from different periods. Although termed 'Old English', Shaw's style also contained elements inspired by holidays on the Continent. The hipped roof overhanging the battlemented bay windows of the West Front, for example, can be found on many French or German castles. In 1884, fifteen years after Shaw started work on the house, it was completed. The final addition was the Drawing Room, in which Armstrong hung the finest of his magnificent collection of paintings (sold some ten years after his death in 1900). Cragside was the first house in the world to be lit by hydroelectricity, installed in 1878. The property is now owned by the National Trust.

NELLY'S MOSS LAKES, CRAGSIDE

In addition to taking an active role in the construction of their country mansion, Cragside, Lord and Lady Armstrong supervised the layout of the grounds (which grew from the original 20 acres to almost 1,730 acres, most of which is now in the care of the National Trust). Being an innovative engineer, Lord Armstrong created a series of lakes to power the hydraulic machinery used by his house and estate. The earliest of Cragside's five lakes was Tumbleton, formed by damming the Debdon Burn. In 1866, Ram House (or Pump House) was built at the base of the dam to house the hydraulic machinery which pumped water to a reservoir above the house. Water from this reservoir then flowed by gravity into the house where it was used for domestic purposes and to power machines such as a hydraulic lift. Nelly's Moss Lakes, fed by the Black Burn, operated a powerful turbine and dynamo installed in the Burnfoot Power House in 1886. The Power House remained in use until 1945, when Cragside was connected to mains electricity.

DEEL'S HILL & BROADSIDE LAW, UPPER COQUETDALE

From its source high in the Cheviot Hills, near the Anglo-Scottish border, the River Coquet meanders westward, past Harbottle Castle, Holystone, Rothbury, Brinkburn Priory and Warkworth, to enter the North Sea at Amble – a journey of some eighty-eight kms (fifty-five miles). Although Upper Coquetdale is traditionally hill-farming country, with sheep predominating over cattle, it lies entirely within the boundary of the Ministry of Defence's Otterburn Training Area. South of the river is a live firing range to which public access is restricted for reasons of security and safety (unexploded ammunition is a very real danger). However, the public have access to rights of way in the area north of the river (shown in the photograph). At the head of the valley are the earthwork remains of the Roman military complex, Chew Green. The nearby stretch of Dere Street, the old Roman road, is known as Gammel's Path. In the sixteenth century, being a busy cross-border point, it was a place where Wardens of the Middle Marches met to settle disputes and maintain the Border Laws.

HARBOTTLE CASTLE, COQUETDALE

Situated on high ground within a loop of the River Coquet, some nineteen kms (twelve miles) upstream of Rothbury, Harbottle Castle was built by Odinel de Umfraville I, Lord of Redesdale, shortly after 1157 to guard the route up the valley into Scotland. Further fortifications were added in the thirteenth century, including a shell keep with projecting towers. It was partially destroyed by the Scots in 1318, and subsequently restored. After James IV of Scotland was killed at Flodden Field in 1513, his widow, Queen Margaret Tudor, married Archibald Douglas, 6th Earl of Angus. In 1515, at Harbottle Castle, she gave birth to a daughter (also called Margaret) who became the grandmother of James VI of Scotland. In 1603, exactly 100 years after his great-grandmother became Queen of Scotland, the Scottish king was crowned James I of England, thereby uniting both countries under a single crown. In 1604 the castle, once the headquarters of the English Warden of the Middle March, was described as 'much decayed'. Some of its stone was used for constructing buildings in Harbottle village.

UPPER COQUETDALE

On the English side of the Anglo-Scottish border, the Cheviot Hills – bounded north and south by the Till valley and Redesdale respectively – are cut by four main river valleys: the College, the Harthope, the Breamish and the Coquet. College valley, running southward from Glendale west of Yeavering Bell, is the most secluded, with limited access to a few motorists along the private road beyond Hethpool. Harthope, running south-westward from Wooler, provides the most popular route to the summit of the Cheviot. Breamish, with a National Park Centre at Ingram, is a favourite place for picnickers. Upper Coquetdale, west of Harbottle, is part of the Ministry of Defence's Otterburn Training Area, covering some 233 square kms (ninety square miles), much of which lies within the bounds of the Northumberland National Park. It is used throughout the year for general army training and large-scale NATO exercises. The two main military camps are at Redesdale and Otterburn. This photograph was taken near Bygate Hall Cottages in Upper Coquetdale.

LADY'S WELL, HOLYSTONE

Hidden amidst a grove of trees, just outside the hamlet of Holystone in Coquetdale, is Lady's Well, so-called because it once belonged to the Augustinian canonesses of Holystone Priory. In his *Comprehensive Guide to Northumberland* (1888), Tomlinson wrote: 'Passing through a rustic arch, surmounted by a cross, the visitor approaches a large quadrangular basin, 39 feet by 24 feet, filled with water of the most crystalline purity. Through a bed of fine sand and gravel the spring bubbles up in numerous small jets, discharging about 16 gallons of water per minute.' Standing in the centre of the holy pool is a cross bearing the worn inscription: 'In this place Paulinus the Bishop baptized 3,000 Northumbrians – Easter DCXXVII [627].' However, according to Tomlinson, 'the venerable bishop was not at Sancta Petra (Holystone) on this Easter-day, but at Sancti Petri (St Peter's Church), York'. The statue outside the pool is said to represent Paulinus. Traditionally, however, the well (now owned by the National Trust) is associated with St Ninian.

BRINKBURN PRIORY

Almost islanded by a loop of the River Coquet, some eight kms (five miles) south-east of Rothbury, Brinkburn Priory was founded between 1130 and 1135 for Augustinian canons by William Bertram I, Baron of Mitford. The first community came from the monastery of St Mary de Insula (probably Pentney Priory in Norfolk). It became an independent, but never wealthy, house in about 1188. The present church, dedicated to St Peter and St Paul, dates from the end of the twelfth century. Subsequent alterations during the medieval period included the addition of two chambers (one over the nave aisle and another over the chancel), plus a sacristy on the north side of the presbytery. These additions were removed during the 1858–9 restoration by Thomas Austin for the then owner, Cadogan Hodgson Cadogan, by which time the church (all that was left of the monastic buildings, apart from that incorp-orated into the nearby house) was a ruin. Now in the care of English Heritage, its style is a fine example of the transition between Norman and Early English architecture.

SIMONSIDE HILLS, FROM LORDENSHAWS

A few kilometres west of Lordenshaws Iron Age hillfort, with its nearby cup-and-ring marked rocks, are the Simonside Hills, predominantly composed of Fell Sandstones. Simonside reaches 1,409 feet (429 metres) above sea-level and nearby Tosson Hill 1,447 feet (441 metres). The hills and forest, including Lordenshaws, can be explored on foot from the old market town of Rothbury, so-called 'Capital of Coquetdale', or from various carparks in the area. Between the town and the hillfort is the prominent circular tower, Sharp's Folly, built by Thomas Sharp, rector of Rothbury between 1720 and 1758, ostensibly to relieve unemployment among local stone masons. It had a practical use, however, as an observatory for studying the stars. Sharp, like other incumbents of Rothbury, lived in nearby Whitton Tower, a fortified rectory, with a pele tower dating back to the fourteenth century. During the lawless times of Border conflict, the rectors' cattle and livestock were secured in the byre on the ground floor, out of sight of marauding reivers.

YEAVERING BELL

Crowning the summit of Yeavering Bell, 1,182 feet (360 metres) above sea-level, are the remains of the largest Iron Age hillfort in Northumberland. In fact, the conical hill has two summits and both are encircled by the stone ramparts of the fort. Within this area of some fifteen acres can be found traces of at least 130 circular huts, together with a Bronze Age cairn. It is thought that the fort was also occupied during the Romano-British period. (The view from the summit in the photograph looks northward, across Glendale, to the hills of the Anglo-Scottish border.) At the foot of Yeavering Bell, near Old Yeavering, is a stone-built monument marking the site of 'Gefrin', the seventh-century country palace of King Edwin of Northumbria (referred to in Bede's *Ecclesiastical History* as 'Adgefrin'). It was here that Paulinus, Bishop of York, was said to have spent thirty-six days doing nothing from dawn to dusk but baptizing converts in the 'cleansing waters of the nearby River Glen'. The site of the palace was identified in 1949 by aerial photography.

HUMBLETON HILL HILLFORT & THE CHEVIOTS

Occupying a commanding site overlooking Wooler and the Milfield Plain, the nine-acre hillfort on Humbleton Hill – 978 feet (298 metres) above sea-level – dates from the Bronze Age and remained in occupation during the Iron Age, and possibly during Roman times. Within the massive stone ramparts are the remains of circular huts. In 1402, on the lower slopes of the hill west of Wooler, the English army under the 1st Earl of Northumberland and his son Sir Henry Percy ('Hotspur') routed the Scots under Archibald, 4th Earl of Douglas. The battle of Humbleton (or Homildon) Hill is mentioned in Shakespeare's *King Henry IV: Part 1*. In that 'sad and bloody hour', according to the bard:

Ten thousand bold Scots, two-and-
    twenty knights,
Balk'd in their own blood.

The battle is commemorated by a stone, near Bendor. Although Archibald and many Scottish nobles were captured, Hotspur refused to surrender them to Henry IV. The quarrel between the Percys and the king culminated in Hotspur's death at Shrewsbury in 1403 – a battle in which Archibald fought on the side of the Percys.

PARISH CHURCH, CHILLINGHAM

The parish church of St Peter at Chillingham, ten kms (six miles) south-east of Wooler, dates from the twelfth century and – despite much alteration and restoration over succeeding centuries – still retains much of its Norman stonework, notably in the nave and chancel. Inside the thirteenth-century chapel of Our Lady, with its little Georgian fireplace, stands an impressive table tomb, the sides of which are decorated with fourteen niches, each containing the figure of a saint (one headless), separated by angels. As these religious figures escaped being destroyed by the iconoclasts of the sixteenth and seventeenth centuries, Pevsner considered the monument to be 'of considerable artistic importance'. The alabaster effigies lying on top of the tomb represent Sir Ralph Grey, who died in 1443, and his wife, Elizabeth. Sir Ralph, his feet resting on a lion, wears a suit of plate armour under a red tabard. Sadly, the dogs at his wife's feet have been badly damaged. Emblems of the Grey family – ladders and cloaks – adorn the monument.

HOUSEY & LANGLEE CRAGS, FROM BLACKSEAT HILL

In the 1720s, Daniel Defoe accompanied by a guide and 'five or six country boys and young fellows', climbed to the summit of the Cheviot. Their route from Wooler was probably up the valley of the Harthope Burn – the stream dividing Blackseat Hill from Housey and Langlee Crags. His ascent by horseback is described in *A Tour Thro' the Whole Island of Great Britain*: 'As we mounted higher we found the hill steeper than at first, also our horses began to complain, and draw their haunches up heavily, so we went very softly: However, we moved still, and went on, till the height began to look really frightful, for, I must own, I wished myself down again.' After managing to reach the top of what Defoe thought was a 'pinnacle' on which they would only have 'room enough to stand, with a precipice every way round', he was surprised to find a flat, smooth summit of 'at least half a mile in diameter; and in the middle of it a large pond, or little lake of water'. At 2,676 feet (816 metres) above sea-level the Cheviot is the highest point in Northumberland.

HARTHOPE VALLEY, FROM HOUSEY CRAGS

Rising on the southern slopes of the flat-topped Cheviot, the Harthope Burn flows north-eastward for some sixteen kms (ten miles) to the old cattle-market town of Wooler, beyond which it merges with the River Till. Below its confluence with the Carey Burn, the stream (having changed its name to the Coldgate Burn) passes through the wooded 'Happy Valley'. Nearer Wooler, the burn changes its name, yet again, to the Wooler Water. In 1791 Sir Walter Scott stayed in the Harthope Valley and wrote to his friend, William Clerk, using a quill from the feather of a crow he had shot for the purpose: 'Behold a letter from the mountains, for I am snugly settled here in a farmer's house about six miles from Wooler in the very centre of the Cheviot Hills in one of the wildest and most romantic situations which your imagination ever suggested...Out of these brooks...we pull trouts of half a yard in length. My uncle drinks the whey here as I do ever since I understood it was brought to his bedside at six every morning by a pretty dairymaid.'

SHEPHERD'S HOUSE, DOD LAW

Rising to a height of over 650 feet (198 metres) above the village of Doddington, in Glendale, is Dod Law – the site of a prehistoric hillfort. This area of moorland is noted for its wealth of cup-and-ring marked rocks. Beside the fort, on the crest of the hill overlooking the River Till, stands the Shepherd's House (referred to by Tomlinson in 1888 as a 'gamekeeper's cottage'). On the hillside below the cottage is 'Cuddy's Cave', named after St Cuthbert. The vertical grooves in the rock nearby are said to have been caused by the Devil. The church in Doddington is unusual in that it underwent a change of orientation in the nineteenth century. Originally the altar was at the east end of the church, but for some unknown reason the interior plan of the building was reversed and it is now at the western end. The watch house in the corner of the churchyard was built in 1826 to deter body-snatching. In the centre of the village are the remains of a bastle or stronghouse, dated 1584. The cross over the 'Bonny Dod Well' was erected by the Earl of Tankerville in 1846.

CHILLINGHAM CASTLE

After obtaining a licence to crenellate in 1344, Sir Thomas Grey converted his thirteenth-century manor house into a rectangular courtyard castle, similar in plan to those at Ford and Etal, with four strong corner towers linked by curtain walls. Despite changes over the centuries, notably during the Elizabethan and Jacobean periods, the stronghold remained essentially medieval until the early seventeenth century, when it was remodelled in a grander style, with the emphasis more on comfort than defence. Further alterations were carried out in 1828 by Sir Jeffrey Wyatville, who was also responsible for laying out the gardens and grounds. Owned by the Earl Grey family and their relations since the thirteenth century, the castle and grounds are open to the public. The park to the east of the village and castle is famous for its herd of Wild White Cattle, a unique and ancient British breed that has survived at Chillingham for at least 700 years. As a precaution, a small reserve herd has been set up in Scotland.

HEPBURN WOOD

Situated at the eastern edge of the moorland plateau, south of Chillingham Park, Hepburn Wood was purchased by the Forestry Commission in 1946. Planted mainly with conifers, the wood is open to the public. Waymarked walks lead to a Bronze Age cist (or grave), dating from 2000 BC, as well as Berthele's Stone (a large rock named after a long-serving Forestry Commission worker and archaeologist). The farming hamlet of Hepburn (shown in the photograph) gave its name to the Hebburn family, who built the nearby bastle house, now a roofless ruin. Pevsner did not consider it 'a bastle in the sense in which the word is now applied, but an oblong stronghouse of the fifteenth century'. The arms of the Hebburns – 'three cressets sable, flaming proper' – are said to represent the beacon (or cresset) which was lit on Ros Castle in times of danger. 'Flaming' may also refer to 'burn' in the family name. 'Hepburn', however, is derived from the Old English for 'high barrow': a reference to the prehistoric burial sites found in the area.

HEPBURN CRAG HILLFORT

Near Chillingham, a circular waymarked walk starts in the Forestry Commission's carpark at Hepburn Wood and, after passing through a conifer plantation, climbs steeply up on to the heather-clad plateau of Hepburn Moor to arrive at Hepburn Crag and the remains of a small prehistoric hillfort. Evidence of another hillfort, in use during the Iron Age, can be found on Ros Castle, the conical hill to the north-east. From the top of this eminence, 1,036 feet (316 metres) above sea-level, there are extensive views over the Northumbrian countryside, the coast and the Cheviot Hills, with Scotland beyond. Ros Castle was once an important beacon site. In 1804, when fears of a French invasion were high, the beacon was lit in error, sparking unnecessary panic throughout the area. In 1936 Ros Castle was presented to the National Trust as part of a memorial to Viscount Grey of Fallodon, Foreign Secretary 1905–16, who, taking Britain into the First World War, said: 'The lamps are going out all over Europe; we shall not see them lit again in our lifetime.'

OLD BEWICK HILLFORT

On the edge of a steep escarpment, overlooking the village of Old Bewick and the valley of the River Breamish, are the earthwork remains of an Iron Age hillfort. In fact, the site contains two horseshoe-shaped forts, placed side by side and enclosed within an outer rampart and ditch. The westernmost fort is considered to be the earliest of the two, and may date from the Bronze Age. Archaeologists are divided about whether the traces inside are of hut circles. The easternmost fort bears the more recent scars of quarrying for millstones. Not far from the earthworks are several rocks with cup-and-ring markings. Describing those on a large stone, ninety metres east of the hillfort, Tomlinson wrote in his *Comprehensive Guide to Northumberland* (1888): 'In spite of the wasting storms of twenty, and it may be thirty centuries, twenty-seven figures are still discernible when the stone is viewed in the light of the evening sun.' At Blawearie, one-and-a-half kms (one mile) north-east of Old Bewick hillfort, are the remains of a Bronze Age burial cairn.

PRESTON TOWER

Dating from the end of the fourteenth century, Preston Tower was erected on a prominent hilltop site – eight kms (five miles) south-west of Seahouses – by Robert Harbottle, the Sheriff of Northumberland and Constable of Dunstanburgh Castle. In 1415 the pele, with walls two metres (seven feet) thick, was mentioned in a list of seventy-eight Border fortresses. Consisting of a rectangular hall with four corner turrets, all that essentially survives of the original structure are the two south turrets and the wall between them. The section of wall on the north side dates from the tower's restoration by Henry Robert Baker-Cresswell in 1864. He also made and installed the clock in the tower. The fifteen-metre (fifty-foot) high tower is open to the public. It contains a guardroom and prison on the ground floor, living accommodation (furnished as it might have been in the year 1400) on the first floor, and an exhibition relating to Border unrest and the battle of Flodden on the second floor. The nearby house, also known as Preston Tower, dates from the early nineteenth century.

ALNWICK CASTLE

The earliest parts of the present Alnwick Castle date back to the end of the eleventh century, when Yvo de Vescy was given the estate by William Rufus. In 1309 the Border stronghold came into the possession of the Percy family, whose descendants (now Dukes of Northumberland) still live there today. Henry, 1st Lord Percy of Alnwick (d. 1315), strengthened much of the castle, including the keep and most of the towers along the curtain wall. The barbican and gatehouse, considered by Pevsner to be 'the best in the country', date from about 1440. When Hugh, 1st Duke of Northumberland, inherited the estate in 1750 the castle was in a state of disrepair. Not only did he commission Robert Adam to remodel the interior in a style that Horace Walpole dismissed as 'gingerbread and snippets of embroidery', he also employed Lancelot 'Capability' Brown to landscape the park. Further restoration to the building was carried out by Anthony Salvin for the 4th Duke in the mid-nineteenth century. The property, with its many treasures, is open to the public.

COQUET ISLAND, FROM AMBLE

Coquet Island lies about one-and-a-half kms (one mile) offshore of the former coal-exporting port of Amble, at the mouth of the River Coquet. It is noted for being the site of a small Benedictine cell, which, according to Bede, was where in 684 Elfleda, Abbess of Whitby, persuaded St Cuthbert to become the Bishop of Lindisfarne. After the Norman Conquest, the monks of Tynemouth Priory also established a small cell on the fourteen-acre island. With their permission, a Danish Christian called Henry settled there to escape marriage and to live as a recluse. Famed for his wisdom, his great insight into people's troubles and his gift of prophecy, St Henry died on the island in 1127 and was buried within the monastic walls at Tynemouth. In about 1540 John Leland wrote: 'The Isle of Coquet standeth upon a very good vein of sea-coal, and at the ebb men dig in the shore by the cliffs, and find very good.' During the Civil War the island was captured and garrisoned by the Scots. In 1841 the lighthouse was built on the remains of the medieval fortified tower.

DUNSTANBURGH CASTLE

In 1313 – fearing Scottish invasion as well as royal reprisal for his part in the 1312 execution of Edward II's homosexual lover, Piers Gaveston – Thomas, 2nd Earl of Lancaster, started to build a powerful fortress on the eminently defensible coastal headland at Dunstanburgh. In 1315, the year following Edward's disastrous defeat at Bannockburn by Robert the Bruce, King of Scotland, Lancaster – supported by the majority of the barons – became virtual ruler of England. Shortly after, Edward granted the earl an official licence to crenellate at Dunstanburgh, thereby giving royal approval for the castle's existence. In 1322, Edward captured Lancaster at the battle of Borough-bridge and, after a summary trial, had him executed as a traitor. By building the largest castle in Northumbria, enclosing some eleven acres, the earl had been able to offer his tenants (with their goods and livestock) a place of refuge in times of danger. The ruins, including a second gatehouse built by John of Gaunt in the 1380s, are now in the care of English Heritage.

WARKWORTH CASTLE

Founded in the middle of the twelfth century, probably as a motte-and-bailey castle, Warkworth Castle occupies a commanding hill-top site overlooking the River Coquet, ten kms (six miles) south-east of Alnwick. The stronghold was acquired by Henry, 2nd Lord Percy of Alnwick, in 1332. As one of the most powerful families in medieval England, often involved in warfare and hostilities, the Percys turned Warkworth into a magnificent fortified residence, with a great keep that was almost a second castle. It was at Warkworth that Henry, 1st Earl of Northumberland, and his son, Harry 'Hotspur' (Sir Henry Percy), are reputed to have hatched the plot to overthrow Henry IV. This rebellion, which culminated in Hotspur's defeat and death at the battle of Shrewsbury in 1403, was immortalized in Shakespeare's *King Henry IV: Part 1*. A short distance upstream from the castle is a hermitage, cut into a cliff beside the river. Its chapel is thought to date from the early fourteenth century. Both castle and hermitage are now in the care of English Heritage.

ALNMOUTH

The origins of Alnmouth date back to at least the Anglo-Saxon period, when a church was built on a hill overlooking the harbour. (It was rebuilt in Norman times and dedicated to St Waleric.) The village is located at the mouth of the River Aln, on what were once the commons of nearby Lesbury. It is some eight kms (five miles) downstream from the castle and abbey at Alnwick, and developed into an important haven for trade and shipping. At the height of its prosperity, in the mid-eighteenth century, the port's main export was corn (many of the large granaries in which the grain was stored were converted into houses in the nineteenth century). Imports included timber and slate. In the 1750s, to stimulate trade even further, a new road (known as the corn road) was constructed between Alnmouth and Hexham. Alnmouth's development as a major port ended dramatically on Christmas Day 1806, when a terrible storm changed the course of the Aln, thereby instigating the gradual decline of the harbour through silting. The same gale also destroyed the Norman church (by then already in ruins).

EDLINGHAM, FROM CORBY'S CRAGS

From Corby's Crags, on the main Rothbury–Alnwick road, this view south-westward towards the ancient hamlet of Edlingham – lying in the narrow valley of the tiny Edlingham Burn, its single street climbing up the partially wooded hillside – includes the remains of the medieval castle, the mainly Norman parish church and the late nineteenth-century railway viaduct (now abandoned). During Victorian times, the Georgian rectory was the scene of an armed robbery for which two Alnwick poachers were wrongly convicted. Although sentenced to penal servitude for life by the judge (who, incidentally, was born in the house), the men were released and pardoned after ten years, when two others finally confessed to the crime. In 1682–3 Edlingham achieved some notoriety when one of its residents, Margaret Stothard, was accused of being a witch. Under oath, John Mills of Edlingham Castle swore that she entered his room in 'a great blast of wind' and materialized at the foot of his bed, only to disappear when he eventually cried 'The Witch the Witch!'.

EDLINGHAM CASTLE

In the first edition of Pevsner's *Buildings of England: Northumberland*, published in 1957, Edlingham Castle was dismissed as 'no more than an ordinary tower-house'. Excavations at the site in 1978–82, however, revealed the existence of a far more complex structure of which the tower was merely one part. In fact, the first stone building – erected by John de Edlingham in the mid-twelfth century – was a two-storey hall house, some thirty metres (100 feet) long by nine metres (thirty feet) wide, with an octagonal turret in each corner (a tall fragment of one of the turrets still survives). As a further defensive measure, the house was surrounded by a moat. The square, three-storey Solar Tower, built by Sir William Felton in the mid-fourteenth century, was erected over the moat (which had been filled). Additional features included a gatehouse, barbican and a range of domestic buildings around a cobbled courtyard. The remains are in the care of English Heritage. The nearby church of St John the Baptist stands on the site of an Anglo-Saxon foundation.

CARLISLE & THE WESTERN BORDER

RIVER EDEN, WARWICK BRIDGE

Near Armathwaite, fourteen kms (nine miles) upstream of Warwick Bridge, an enigmatic series of round, staring faces have been carved in the sandstone cliffs. Nearby is a salmon and several lines adapted from Izaak Walton's *The Compleat Angler* (1653):

OH THE FISHERS GENTLE LIFE
HAPPIEST IS OF ANY VOID OF PLEASURE,
FULL OF STRIFE AND BELOVED BY
MANY. OTHER JOYS ARE BUT TOYS
AND TO BE LAMENTED ONLY THIS A
PLEASURE IS TIMBER ★ FISHING.

Some words have letters missing and some letters have been carved back to front. Dated 1855 and initialled 'I. B.', the lines may have been carved by members of the Mounsey family of Castleton House, Rockcliffe, on a fishing expedition. The origin and date of the faces is unknown. In 1850 William Mounsey walked the entire 120 kms (seventy-five miles) of the Eden, from his home near the river's entry into the Solway, to its source high on Mallerstang Common. The marble monument near Hugh Seat, which commemorated his achievement, was destroyed in 1870.

Occupying a natural defensive position on a bluff overlooking crossing-points of the rivers Eden and Caldew, and almost on the border with Scotland, Carlisle Castle was of such strategic importance during medieval times that it was described as 'the key to England'. Although William Rufus claimed Carlisle as part of England in 1092, both city and castle suffered frequent attacks by successive Scottish kings, all anxious to regain control of the disputed territory. Despite notable assaults by William the Lion in 1173–4 and Robert Bruce in 1315, Carlisle was held by the Scots between only 1135 and 1157 – the period which almost exactly coincided with the civil war between King Stephen and the Empress Maud. Nevertheless, the castle was captured by the Parliamentarians (some of whom were Scots) during the Civil War and also, briefly, in 1745 by the invading army of Charles Edward Stuart (Bonnie Prince Charlie).

In 1284, having successfully conquered Wales, Edward I turned his attention to uniting the kingdoms of England and Scotland under his personal rule. The ruthless campaigns he waged against the people north of the Border earned him the nickname 'Hammer of the Scots'. When Alexander III, King of Scotland, died in 1286, he left his granddaughter, the three-year-old Margaret, 'Maid of Norway', as his heir. Until she came of age, six guardians of the realm were appointed as regents to govern Scotland. In an attempt to increase the power of his family, Edward arranged for Margaret to marry his son, Prince Edward (later Edward II). On the voyage from Norway in September 1290, Margaret was taken ill and died. Her death not only put an end to Edward's son becoming King of Scotland, it also sparked off fierce contention over who should succeed to the Scottish throne. Unable to settle the issue amongst themselves, the Scottish nobles invited Edward to arbitrate between the two main claimants, John Baliol and Robert Bruce. He agreed on the understanding that they recognized him as feudal overlord of Scotland. Before declaring Baliol king in 1292, however, Edward managed to get the Scots to surrender all their castles to English occupying forces. Over time, the continual humiliation of having to settle Scottish disputes in English courts led Baliol to rebel. Mounting tension between the two countries often erupted

into small-scale battles. (It was during one such skirmish that Sir Malcolm Wallace, father of William Wallace – see below – was killed.) In desperation, Baliol appealed to Philip IV, King of France, for help in driving the English out of Scotland. The Franco-Scottish alliance against England, formed in 1295 (later known as the 'Auld Alliance'), lasted until 1560 when it was renounced by Scotland.

Edward I responded to Baliol's bid for independence by invading Scotland in 1296. After sacking Berwick-upon-Tweed and slaughtering thousands of men, women and children, the English army marched to Dunbar where it defeated the Scots in battle on 27 April. Shortly after, in a deliberately symbolic act, the coronation stone of Scone, the Stone of Destiny, was taken to Westminster Abbey – where it remained (except when stolen in 1950–52) until its ceremonial return to Scotland in November 1996. Having forced Baliol to surrender his kingdom, Edward received the formal homage of some two thousand Scottish nobles, and his conquest of Scotland seemed complete.

William Wallace, however, had other plans. After leading guerrilla attacks against the English, including ambushing and slaying the knight who had killed his father, Wallace attracted an increasing number of followers. His dramatic victory over the English army at the battle of Stirling Bridge on 11 September 1297 ignited widespread rebellion. One Scottish fortress after another surrendered to Wallace's seemingly invincible forces. In October the Scots invaded England, ravaged a huge swathe of countryside and returned home laden with booty. The only stronghold the Scots decided to stop and besiege in their sweeping onslaught across Northumbria was Carlisle Castle – the western gateway to Scotland. The siege was eventually abandoned because of lack of provisions. As an act of revenge, Sir Robert Clifford mounted a ruthless campaign from Carlisle into Scotland, burning several towns and villages, including Annan. Whilst anarchy prevailed in Scotland and the Borderlands, Edward I was overseas in Flanders, fighting the French under Philip IV.

Early in 1298, Wallace – having sworn fealty to his king in exile, John Baliol – was knighted and appointed 'Guardian of Scotland'. After negotiating a truce with France, Edward returned to England to find his army ready to march north against the Scots. On 22 June 1298 the opposing forces met near Falkirk. During the ensuing battle the Scottish cavalry fled the field. Despite standing firm for a long time, Wallace and the remainder of his followers eventually succumbed to the deadly hail of arrows from Edward's longbowmen. Defeat turned into a rout, with Wallace barely managing to escape with his life. After a period of exile in France, Wallace returned to Scotland to resume harrying the English. He was captured by an act of betrayal in 1305 and taken to Carlisle Castle, from where he was escorted to London for trial.

CARLISLE CATHEDRAL

Although St Cuthbert is known to have visited a monastery at Carlisle in 686, its exact location is unknown – not surprisingly, for during the ninth century the town was completely destroyed by the Danes. In *The History of the County of Cumberland* (1794), Hutchinson wrote: 'So complete was the destruction, that she [Carlisle] lay overwhelmed in her desolation, till the time of William the Conqueror, when one of his followers [Walter, a wealthy Norman priest] is said to have rebuilt some parts of the city, founded, or restored the ancient religious society there, and dedicated the house to the honour of the Blessed Virgin, of which he became chief.' Henry I replaced Walter's foundation with an Augustinian priory and, in 1133, the priory church was made a cathedral. The history of the building thereafter is beset with damage, either from serious fires or from attacking armies. Its last major restoration was undertaken during Victorian times. The great east window, retaining some of its original fourteenth-century glass, was also renovated.

Found guilty of treason and other crimes, Wallace was dragged through the streets to the place of his execution. There he was hung, drawn and quartered.

The following year, Robert Bruce rebelled, murdered his rival John Comyn and then had himself crowned Robert I, King of Scots. On 7 July 1307, Edward I died of illness while marching north from Carlisle with his army. His son, Edward II, was decisively beaten by the Scots, under Bruce, at the battle of Bannockburn in 1314. For centuries thereafter, the Anglo-Scottish frontier remained in a state of turmoil, with not only armies, but highly organized bands of raiders (reivers) terrorizing the inhabitants of the region. Lawlessness prevailed, especially in the 'Debatable Land' – the narrow strip of land, some six kms (four miles) wide and nineteen kms (twelve miles) long, north-east of the city of Carlisle. As the area did not come under the control and jurisdiction of either England or Scotland, criminals and outlaws used it as a base from which to launch raids on the inhabitants of both countries. One attempt to discourage people from settling in the Debatable Land was to declare that robbery, murder and, indeed, any other crime could be committed within the area without fear of punishment. When ownership of this long-disputed frontier land was finally settled in 1552 (by its division into two, with the larger portion going to the Scots) the inhabitants apparently celebrated by a renewed outbreak of raiding.

To try and establish some kind of law and order in the region, the Anglo-Scottish Borderlands were divided into six Marches, three in England and three in Scotland. Each March was placed under the jurisdiction of a Warden, who was expected to settle Border disputes and uphold Border Law (a code of practice unique to the frontier region). Wardens, appointed by their respective governments, met regularly on 'March Days'. Meetings that should have been peaceful often ended in violence since many of the Wardens were involved in reiving activities themselves. One legal way for a person to recover goods and livestock stolen in a raid was by immediate pursuit, known as 'hot trod'. In order for the trod to be lawful, the pursuers had to set out within three days of the raid (while the trail was still 'hot') and brandish a piece of burning turf held aloft on the point of a lance. It was the duty of all able-bodied men between the ages of sixteen and sixty to join the trod. Refusal brought harsh penalties. Reivers caught 'red handed' could expect 'Jeddart Justice' (to be executed first and tried later). Not surprisingly, therefore, they went armed with lances, swords and later hand guns in readiness for both attack and defence. They also wore protective clothing, notably steel bonnets and padded jackets (jacks). Taking part in a hot trod, despite its legality, was a risky venture, with little guarantee of success.

In a time of 'take or have taken, kill or be killed,' strength, safety and survival lay in belonging to a powerful Border family (known as the Surname, clan or grayne). As families fought and stole from each other, often in alliance with other families, deadly feuds were common. Those families that raided together were known as the Riding Surnames. Reiving usually took place at night between October and March. Those farmers and smallholders who did not belong to a powerful Surname could not expect the law to protect them from raiders. Instead, they were forced to pay the professional reivers protection money or blackmail ('black rent'), to be left alone.

The daring exploits and bloody feuds of the reivers were handed down from generation to generation in the form of dialect folksongs, or 'Border Ballads', many of which were collected in the early nineteenth century by Sir Walter Scott. However, being a writer, he was not averse to 'improving' them and adding new ones of his own. The ballad of *Kinmont Willie* tells the story of the notorious reiver, William Armstrong, who led a gang of villains from the Debatable Land, known as 'Kinmont's Bairns'. In 1596, Kinmont was returning home from a Truce Day when he was captured by the deputy Warden of the English West March and imprisoned in Carlisle Castle. Since he had been taken in Liddesdale, the Keeper, Walter Scott of Buccleuch (nicknamed 'Bold Buccleuch'), demanded Kinmont's immediate release on the basis that he had been unlawfully arrested during a day of truce. Having tried and failed to secure the release of the reiver by peaceful means, Buccleuch decided to rescue him by force. Leading a band of some two hundred Riding Surnames – Grahams, Scotts, Armstrongs and Elliots – he managed to enter the castle, free Kinmont Willie and get him safely away into Scotland. Tradition says that Elizabeth I was so furious when told of the incident that she ordered Buccleuch to appear before her to explain his actions. When asked how he dared to break into her royal castle, Bold Buccleuch replied: 'What, madam, is there that a brave man may not dare?' At this point the Queen's anger evaporated and he was allowed to return home free of any punishment.

Soon after King James VI of Scotland became James I of England in 1603, it was deemed that a frontier between the two countries was no longer necessary. The name of the Border counties was changed to the Middle Shires and the system of Wardens and March Law abolished. The enormous, practical task of pacifying the region followed: first by demolishing the reivers' strongholds, then by taking away their weapons and armour, and finally by subjecting them to the same laws as the rest of the kingdom. For the families who had survived for centuries by plunder and pillage, it meant the end of a whole way of life. Many, therefore, decided to resist. But, deprived of the Border and its special laws, the rebels found themselves fighting a hopeless cause. The authorities were adamant that everyone had to conform to the ordinary law of the land. Those who refused were either executed or banished overseas. The death penalty awaited anyone who returned from exile. Bold Buccleuch helped in the task of pacification by taking some two thousand Scots to the Low Countries to fight as mercenaries against Spain. But old ways die hard and peace in the Borders was still some way off. Gradually, a new kind of raider – not as violent as the reivers – appeared in the wilder, mossier and boggier parts of the Borderlands. Known as 'mosstroopers', they were particularly active during and after the Civil War.

Shortly after the relatively bloodless invasion of England by the Dutch Protestant prince, William of Orange, in November 1688, King James II, a Roman Catholic and a Stuart, was forced to abdicate and flee to France. In April the following year, William and his wife Mary (daughter of James II) were jointly crowned at Westminster on the sworn undertaking that they would promote the Protestant religion and restore civil liberties. The supporters of James, known as Jacobites, rose up in outrage, instigating a campaign to restore the Stuarts to the throne that went on to last for over fifty years. The two major Jacobite rebellions occurred in 1715 and 1745 (the latter led by James II's grandson, Bonnie Prince Charlie). Both failed. After defeat at the battle of Culloden in April 1746, Charles fled the country leaving his supporters to suffer the wrath of English retribution. Almost four hundred Jacobites were tried and gruesomely executed at Carlisle. It was said that even the hardened inhabitants of the city were so sickened by the slaughter that they retreated to their homes in disgust. According to some, the words of the song 'The Bonnie Banks of Loch Lomond' were inspired by the lament of one of the Scottish prisoners. When he said to his true love, 'Ye'll take the high road and I'll take the low road and I'll be in Scotland afore ye', what he meant (according to popular belief) was that after death his soul would travel home underground.

Following the defeat of the Stuarts, the next revolution in Northumbria would be the one that transformed the North-East into an industrial centre of world importance.

CARLISLE CASTLE

Some thirty-five years after their successful invasion of England in AD 43, the Romans established a military base at *Luguvalium* (Carlisle), on the southern banks of the River Eden, from which they planned to conquer Scotland. The fort was demolished during the construction of Hadrian's Wall and its garrison moved north across the river to the key fort of *Uxelodunum* (Stanwix). Thereafter, the civil settlement developed into a walled city covering over seventy acres, and probably into a *civitas* (the tribal capital of the Carvetii). In 1092, William Rufus recaptured Carlisle from the Scots (who had held it since the tenth century) and built a motte-and-bailey castle on the site of the first Roman fort. He also fortified the city, the walls of which were strengthened during the reign of his brother, Henry I. Between 1135 and 1157 the castle was in Scottish hands. Thereafter, it was attacked by the Scots many times until the defeat of the Stuarts at Culloden in 1746. The castle's oldest stone building is the keep, begun in the 1120s.

EDWARD I MONUMENT, BURGH-BY-SANDS

In 1685, on the broad, desolate and level pastures of Burgh Marsh, just over one-and-a-half kms (one mile) north of the village of Burgh-by-Sands, Henry Howard, 7th Duke of Norfolk, erected a pillar to mark the spot where Edward I died on 7 July 1307. It fell down in 1795 and was replaced by the present monument, erected by William Lowther, 1st Earl of Lonsdale of the 2nd creation, in 1803. Standing within a railed enclosure, it consists of a square sandstone column, about six metres (twenty feet) high, surmounted by a cross. One side of the monument bears an inscription commemorating Edward, while another records its restoration by the 4th Earl of Lonsdale in 1876. Nicknamed 'Hammer of the Scots' because of the ruthless campaigns he waged to conquer Scotland, Edward I camped with his army on Burgh Marsh in 1307, near a convenient ford across the Solway only passable at low tide. After leaving Lanercost Priory, where he had lain ill for five months during the previous winter, his health slowly deteriorated. His death brought the planned invasion of Scotland to an abrupt end.

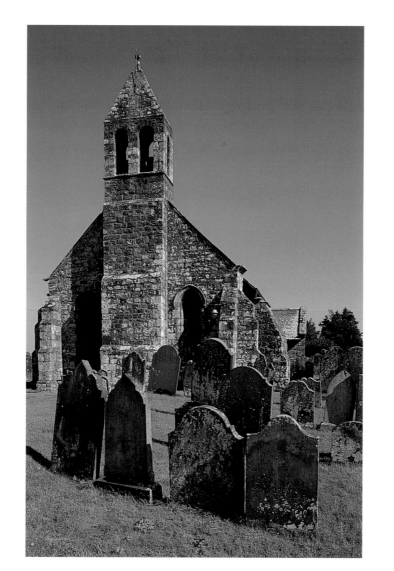

PARISH CHURCH, BOWNESS-ON-SOLWAY

Although the western extremity of Hadrian's Wall was the Roman fort of *Maia* or *Maium* (Bowness-on-Solway), coastal defences continued south to Maryport, and possibly St Bees Head. In his *Practical Guide to Carlisle, Gilsland, Roman Wall, & Neighbourhood* (1875) Jenkinson wrote of Bowness: 'a small quiet old village, composed of a few farmsteads, lodging-houses, and fishermen's cottages; but containing few traces of the Roman city which once existed here. The inhabitants appear to know little of the old Romans, but they are well informed as to the Salmon Fisheries Act, and can argue ably and with feeling on the injustice of allowing the standing engines and nets to be used on the Scottish side, and within sight, whilst they are deprived of them. We cannot but sympathize with them, for such an anomaly certainly seems unfair.' The restored parish church of St Michael, dating from Norman times, was mainly built with stones from the Roman fort. At Port Carlisle, one-and-a-half kms (one mile) to the east, a harbour, linked to Carlisle by a canal, was built in 1819–23. The enterprise failed.

BIRDOSWALD ROMAN FORT, NEAR GILSLAND

Because of its position high on an escarpment above a loop in the River Irthing, the Romans named the fort at Birdoswald on Hadrian's Wall *Banna*, meaning 'a spur' or 'a tongue'. In *The History of the County of Cumberland* (1794) Hutchinson wrote: 'The situation of this station is excellent, on a large plain, which terminates with a steep descent towards the river; the eminence gives it command of prospect over the adjacent country; and the ascent of the plain on every hand, at some little distance from the fort, gave it great natural strength.' From the point where it crossed the River Irthing to Bowness-on-Solway, Hadrian's Wall was originally built of turf. In order to accommodate the later stone fort of *Banna*, part of the turf wall was demolished. When the turf was replaced by stone, the line of the wall was moved from the east and west sides of the fort to the northern corners. A military road also linked Birdoswald with Bewcastle. For centuries until 1984, when it was acquired by Cumbria County Council, Birdoswald was the home of farmers.

LANERCOST PRIORY

Founded for Augustinian canons in about 1166 by Robert de Vaux (or Vallibus), Lanercost Priory was endowed with various tracts of land, including a long stretch of the Irthing valley between the river and Hadrian's Wall, on which the monastery was built. The canons also received income from five parish churches – Irthington, Brampton, Carlatton, Farham and Walton. The monastic church, dedicated to St Mary Magdalene, was completed by about 1220. Being close to the turbulent Anglo-Scottish border, the peace of the house was often shattered, either by marauding raiders or by being treated as a military headquarters. In 1296 and 1297, to mention but two instances, the house was robbed and despoiled by Scottish armies, first under John Comyn, Earl of Buchan, and then under William Wallace. King Edward I, Queen Eleanor and their huge household stayed several times at the priory, the last time being for five months in 1306–7. The ruins are now in the care of English Heritage whilst the monastic nave serves as the parish church.

CHURCH & CASTLE, BEWCASTLE

In addition to Hadrian's Wall, the Romans erected a number of forward front-line forts from which they could patrol the hostile territory to the north. The outpost fort at Bewcastle, built on a low hill above the Kirk Beck, was unusually six-sided. Its name *Fanum Cocidi* means 'the temple of Cocidius'. Silver plaques and stone altars dedicated to Cocidius, a Celtic war god, have been discovered at the site and the Romans may have built the fort over an already existing shrine. In the late seventh or early eighth century a beautifully carved sandstone cross was erected within the Roman fortifications. Today, the Bewcastle Cross still stands in its original position and, despite the loss of its cross-head, is one of the most impressive monuments to survive from the days of early Christianity in Northumbria. Although rebuilt in 1792 and completely renovated in 1901, the parish church of St Cuthbert contains evidence of earlier foundations. The ruins of the medieval castle stand in the north-east corner of the Roman fort.

ROTHERHOPE FELL, ALSTON MOOR

After describing his fearful experience of being caught in a sudden snowstorm on the high moors near Alston, Walter White wrote: 'Very different is this wild hill-country in summer: though bleak and barren it then shows whatever it has of beauty and sunshine; and there is beauty in the wide rolling expanse, in the great brown heathy slopes here and there broken by rocks and screes, and grouped in varying outline where they plunge upon the valleys. The eye roving afar detects alternations of colour; perceives an almost forest-like effect in the shadows of clouds, and rests fondly on the patches of green which denote the outburst of spring, or the bestowal of culture.' The streams that rise on Rotherhope Fell (part of Alston Moor) flow north to feed the rivers Black Burn and South Tyne (both of which meet at Bleagate). From the bleak upland wilderness of Cross Fell, reaching 2,920 feet (890 metres) above sea-level, the Pennine Way heads north-eastward to the lesser heights of Rotherhope Fell, before descending to Garrigill in the South Tyne valley.

ALSTON, FROM PENNINE WAY

At about 1,000 feet (300 metres) above sea-level, Alston, on the Pennine Way, is the highest market town in England and a popular base for exploring the North Pennines. In 1859 Walter White wrote: 'The principal street is so steep that you will pant again while on the way through the market-place to the upper part of the town, and perhaps incline to stop and look at the queer hard-featured houses and the curious shops, among which there is a good display of mining gear and implements. Truly just such a town as you would expect to see, which has long been the isolated metropolis of the mining region, which for want of good roads was difficult of access until 1828, when by aid of McAdam, the road-maker, and a stage coach, the town was brought into daily communication with Penrith and Newcastle. Now, by a branch line to Haltwhistle, it connects with the Newcastle and Carlisle railway.' Although the line closed in 1976, part of the route from Alston has been reopened by the South Tyneside Railway Preservation Society.

FARMHOUSE, GARRIGILL

In his *Practical Guide to Carlisle, Gilsland, Roman Wall, & Neighbourhood* (1875), Jenkinson wrote of the area around Alston, Nenthead and Garrigill, then a busy lead-mining centre: 'The inhabitants of these mining dales are very civil and intelligent, but the stranger will sometimes receive a reply in an unknown tongue, unless his Celtic education has been attended to. Compulsory education is not new here. The London Lead Mining Company have always required their workmen to send their children both to day and Sunday school...The rude old farmhouses are often very picturesque without, sheltered by a few aged beeches or sycamores, but within they bear testimony to a very rough way of life...The hum of the spinning-wheel may still be occasionally heard, as the frugal housewife spins the self-grey wool into stockings, unequalled for comfort and wear. But these old houses are fast being altered or rebuilt, and many of the primitive customs of an hospitable race are passing away.' Many rare plants can be found growing wild in the locality today.

SOUTH TYNE VALLEY, NEAR TYNE HEAD

The River Tyne boasts two distinctly separate sources: the North Tyne which rises on Deadwater Moor in the Kielder Forest; and the South Tyne which starts life on the peaty moorland around Tyne Head in the North Pennines. The latter flows in a north-easterly arc past Garrigill, Alston, Lambley, Haltwhistle and Haydon Bridge, before joining the North Tyne near Hexham. During medieval times, the 'Silver Mines of Carlisle' were located around Alston Moor and Tyne Head. The silver content of the lead from these early mines was so high that it was used by the Royal Mint in Carlisle. In the late eighteenth and nineteenth centuries the area was one of the most productive lead-mining centres in Europe. A rare vein of gold was even rumoured to exist near Tyne Head. Evidence of past workings litter the hillsides. In addition to spoil heaps and abandoned mines, there are the ruins of the former mining hamlet of Tynehead and the remains of kilns used by the miner-farmers to produce lime to improve the fertility of their moorland fields.

NENTHEAD MINES, NEAR ALSTON

Once an important centre for the mining and smelting of lead, zinc and silver, the village of Nenthead is made up of five distinct areas: Overwater, Holmesfoot, Whitehall, Hilltop and Hillersdon Terrace. Situated some 1,500 feet (450 metres) above sea-level, near the source of the River Nent (a tributary of the South Tyne), the settlement is one of the highest in England. Indeed, the Church of St John the Evangelist, built in 1845, claims to be 'the highest parish church in England'. The village owes its development to the Quaker-owned London Lead Company, which not only mined and smelted at Nenthead during the eighteenth and nineteenth centuries, but also looked after its workers' welfare by providing shops, chapels and houses, together with the country's first free lending library and compulsory schooling. Furthermore, the Company did not try to impose the Quaker religion on its employees; instead they were encouraged to follow the denomination of their choice. Today, the village's history can be explored in the Nenthead Mines Heritage Centre.

PARISH CHURCH, KIRKOSWALD

Standing beside an ancient holy spring at the foot of Bell Tower Hill, the present church of St Oswald dates from Norman times, and is rumoured to be connected to the castle (now ruined) by an underground passage. The first church to stand on the site was founded in the seventh century, after St Oswald and St Aidan discovered pagans worshipping at the spring, and converted them to Christianity. The bell tower, rebuilt in 1893, was sited on the top of the hill so that the bells could be clearly heard by the villagers. North-west of Kirkoswald are the 'Nunnery Walks', laid out in *c.*1775 by Christopher Aglionby along the banks of Croglin Beck. In *The History of the County of Cumberland* (1794), Hutchinson wrote of the walks: 'Though confined, the views are wild and picturesque:- romantic and unrivalled beauties attract the attention of all strangers, and the admiration of every one who has taste to admire nature in those forms, where the grand, the sublime, the romantic, and the beautiful are all united.'

LONG MEG & HER DAUGHTERS, LITTLE SALKELD

Occupying rising ground on the east side of the Eden valley, some ten kms (six miles) north-east of Penrith, are the remains of an extensive ceremonial complex dating from the late Neolithic to Early Bronze Age. Local legend says that a witch, known as Long Meg, was turned to stone together with her followers for dancing on the Sabbath. Long Meg (a tall red sandstone monolith) stands some eighteen metres (sixty feet) south-west of her 'Daughters' (a large stone circle, composed of boulders of volcanic porphyrite, part of which is shown in this photograph). Among the motifs on Long Meg's side are cup-and-ring marks, thought to have been carved over four thousand years ago. In his *Monumenta Britannica: A Miscellany of British Antiquities*, compiled mainly between 1665 and 1693, John Aubrey quotes Sir William Dugdale: 'in the middle [of the circle] are two tumuli, or barrows of cobble-stones, nine or ten foot high'. No trace of them exists today. Aubrey also mentioned that 'a giant's bone and body' were discovered in 'the middle of the orbicular stones'. The name 'Meg' may derive from 'magus', meaning 'magician'.

LACY'S CAVES, LITTLE SALKELD

After visiting 'Long Meg and her Maidens', near Little Salkeld, Walter White set out to see Lacy's Caves, on the east bank of the Eden. In *Northumberland & the Border* (1859) he wrote: 'Then we found a way down a broad deep gulley, through tall rank grass, and amid thickly-growing oaks, to the brink of the Eden, near a red sandstone bluff, in which are the Lacy Caves; so named from a resident in the neighbour-hood, who undertook their excavation. You will find arched passages receding into the darkness, and with an outlook from sundry openings upon the stream, admirable for their environment, if not for themselves. The river is broad and clear, makes a bend round the hill, tumbles with rush and roar over a stony mill dam, the bank is steep and wooded, a rill runs across with lively babble; and these make up a happy finish to a morning's walk.' Named after Samuel Lacy, who owned Salkeld Hall in the eighteenth century, the caves are thought to have been modelled on the ancient caves of St Constantine's Cell, downstream at Wetheral.

CASTLE KEEP, APPLEBY-IN-WESTMORLAND

Occupying a strategic position on the ancient route from the Vale of York over the Pennines to Carlisle and Scotland, the market town of Appleby grew up in a loop of the River Eden under the shadow of the Norman castle. The manorial lord's bondsmen (unfree tenants) lived in Bongate, on the opposite (eastern) side of the river – probably the site of the pre-Norman settlement. The medieval bridge connecting both areas was replaced in 1889. Typically, the Norman town was laid out on a simple defensive plan with a wide enclosed area (Boroughgate) stretching from the church to the castle. Access to this central market area was through narrow, easily blocked passages. In 1174, the year the town and castle were sacked by William the Lion, Henry II elevated Appleby to the status of a Royal Borough (confirmed by his 1179 charter). Today, Appleby Castle is privately owned, but its grounds – including the twelfth-century keep and a collection of rare-breed farm animals, birds and waterfowl – are open to the public during the tourist season.

PARISH CHURCH, APPLEBY-IN-WESTMORLAND

Standing at the foot of the long, wide market street of Boroughgate, the parish church of St Lawrence at Appleby dates from the establishment of the town and castle in Norman times. At Bongate, on the opposite side of the river, St Michael's (now a private residence) contains evidence of an earlier foundation. Like the town, both churches suffered repeated damage from Border raids. St Lawrence was virtually destroyed by the Scots in 1174, and again in 1388. The present building (preserving the bottom part of the twelfth-century west tower) is in two medieval styles: internally mostly Decorated and externally Perpendicular. Like St Michael's, the church was extensively restored by Lady Anne Clifford in the middle of the seventeenth century. Lady Anne lived at the castle (which she restored in 1653) and, after her death in 1676, was buried in the church near the monument to her mother, Margaret, Countess of Cumberland. She also founded St Anne's Hospital (thirteen almshouses and a chapel), on the east side of Boroughgate.

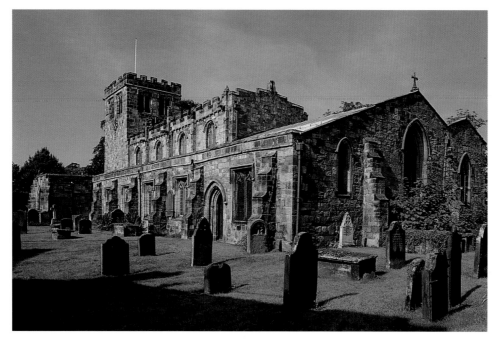

BROUGH CASTLE

After the Conquest, the Normans erected castles at Brough and Appleby-in-Westmorland to guard the invasion route from Scotland down the Eden valley and over the Stainmore Pass to the Vale of York. The earliest stone castle at Brough was erected in about 1100 on the northern third of the Roman fort of *Verteris*. Although William the Lion, King of Scotland, failed to take Carlisle during his invasion of 1174, his army did manage to capture and destroy the castles at both Appleby and Brough. Brough Castle was rebuilt towards the end of the century by Theobald de Valoines. He is thought to have built the present keep, but it may have been erected by Robert de Vipont (Vieuxpont), who was granted the barony by King John in 1203 and subsequently rebuilt the gatehouse. The round tower was built by Robert Clifford, who acquired half of the Vipont estates at the end of the thirteenth century. Brough Castle remained in the Clifford family until the death of Lady Anne Clifford in 1676. The ruins are now in the care of English Heritage.

DURHAM & THE SOUTH-EASTERN BORDER

WEARDALE, FROM WHITE HALL

Although designated an Area of Outstanding Natural Beauty, Weardale, like many other dales in the North Pennines, still bears the scars of at least eight centuries of lead mining. The industry, which reached its peak during the latter half of the nineteenth century, rapidly declined due to the availability of cheaper, imported ores from overseas. Today, the rich heritage of Weardale's long-abandoned lead-mining industry has been preserved at the Killhope Lead Mining Centre. Further information on the history of the area can be found at the Weardale Museum at Ireshopeburn, including a collection of minerals, rocks and fossils and a working model of a local lead mine. Founded in 1985, the museum is housed in the old manse, adjoining the eighteenth-century High House Chapel where John Wesley, the founder of Methodism, often preached. The village of Frosterley gives its name to a decorative 'marble', formed from a black, carboniferous limestone, which can be found in many local churches, including Durham Cathedral.

During the latter half of the eighteenth and first half of the nineteenth centuries, the Industrial Revolution irreversibly transformed the landscape and society of much of Britain. By the time the transformation was complete, the nation was predominantly industrial rather than agricultural; with most people living in towns rather than in the country, and most goods being produced by machine rather than by hand. The triangle of eastern Northumbria, centred on Durham and lying between the mouths of the rivers Coquet and Tees, contained large deposits of surface and underground coal – a fossil fuel used for driving steam engines and (in the form of coke) smelting iron. In consequence, the area attracted industrial development on an unprecedented scale.

Minerals were mined long before the Romans burned coal for heat, smelted iron for weapons and used lead for pipes, cisterns and baths. Yet the earliest documented evidence of coal, iron and lead mining in Northumbria dates from medieval times when all three minerals were exploited by the monasteries, as well as by the Prince Bishops of Durham. At first, coal was picked up on the Northumbrian seashore or dug out of exposed seams on the hillside. Later, especially after the invention and introduction of steam-driven pumps and engines, it was extracted from deep underground, even from under the seabed. From at least the thirteenth century, 'sea-coal' (as it was known in the south of England) was being shipped from Northumbria to London, where pollution (in the form of dense fog) from burning the fuel created problems that remained unresolved for centuries.

In *The History of England* (1880), Lord Macaulay wrote of the 'State of England in 1685', before the dawn of the Industrial Revolution:

Coal, though very little used in any species of manufacture, was already the ordinary fuel in some districts which were fortunate enough to possess large beds, and in the capital, which could easily be supplied by water carriage. It seems reasonable to believe that at least half of the quantity then extracted from the pits was consumed in London. The consumption of London seemed to the writers of that age enormous, and was often mentioned by them as a proof of the greatness of the imperial city. They scarcely hoped to be believed when they affirmed that two hundred and eighty thousand chaldrons, that is to say, about three hundred and fifty thousand tons, were, in the last year of the reign of Charles the Second, brought to the Thames. At present three millions and a half of tons are required yearly by the metropolis; and the whole annual produce cannot, on the most moderate consumption, be estimated at less than thirty millions of tons.

Daniel Defoe visited the North-East in the early eighteenth century, and wrote in *A Tour Thro' the Whole Island of Great Britain*:

> The road to Newcastle gives a view of the inexhausted store of coals and coal pits, from whence not London only, but all the south part of England is continually supplied; and whereas when we are at London, and see the prodigious fleets of ships which come constantly in with coals for this increasing city, we are apt to wonder whence they come, and that they do not bring the whole country away.

Although iron ore, zinc, barytes and fluorspar, and even small deposits of coal, can be found in the North Pennines, west of the Durham and Northumberland coalfields, it was the presence of rich veins of lead that caused a mining boom in the eighteenth and nineteenth centuries. The two main businesses operating in the North Pennines were the Quaker-run London Lead Company and W. B. Lead, owned by the Blackett (later Beaumont) family: the former concentrating on workings in Teesdale and on Alston Moor, and the latter on mining in Weardale and the Allendales. It is estimated that at its peak W. B. Lead produced some twenty-five per cent of the total lead mined in England. At Killhope, in Upper Weardale, the company leased the mining rights from the Bishop of Durham. After the collapse of the industry due to cheaper foreign imports, the Killhope mine continued to be worked until 1910. It finally closed after being re-opened briefly in 1916.

Today, Killhope Lead Mining Centre, owned by Durham County Council, is acclaimed as the best-preserved lead-mining site in Britain. In addition to exploring the buildings on the surface – which include a fully mechanized crushing and separation plant powered by a water-wheel over ten metres (thirty-three feet) in diameter – visitors can descend deep underground, where a smaller waterwheel was installed to pump water to the surface. Life for the lead miner (most of whom were also farmers) was harsh and dangerous. Those who survived being killed or maimed by explosions or accidents, often succumbed to early death through lung disease or lead poisoning. Many were old men by the age of fifty-five. Occasionally, a miner would break through into long-abandoned levels. These workings, as well as the unknown people who had made them, were known as 'the old man'. On more than one occasion in the Park Level Mine at Killhope, a miner would think that he had discovered a rich, new vein, only to have his hopes dashed when he found 'the old man' had been there before him.

One major development of the Industrial Revolution was the arrival of the railways, encouraged by engineers like George Stephenson and his son, Robert. Despite the establishment of a 'modern' waterway network, which started with the construction of the Bridgewater Canal in the 1760s, freight and passenger transport was almost entirely dominated by rail during the Victorian period. Wooden-railed, horse-drawn wagonways, linking mines with waterways, were first introduced to Northumbria by about 1605. Indeed, during the late eighteenth and early nineteenth centuries, one such wagonway ran right past George Stephenson's Birthplace at Wylam, on the River Tyne. The company formed by George and his son, Robert, was responsible for building the world's first public railway to use steam locomotion. Running for some sixteen kms (ten miles) between the two Teesside towns of Stockton and Darlington, the line was opened in 1825. Their historic engine, the 'Locomotion', is now on display in the Darlington Railway Centre and Museum, housed in the original Darlington station. The widespread development of the railway network led to a dramatic fall in the price of transporting freight, notably coal.

At the beginning of the twentieth century almost one-quarter of the working population of the Durham area were directly employed in coal mining. In turn, cheap and readily available coal encouraged the development of coal-using industries, notably chemicals and engineering. The increased demand for iron and steel for railways increased the demand for coal, which, in turn, stimulated the demand for ships. Growth spiralled, turning the north-east of England into one of the great industrial centres of the world. Then, after the First World War, demand for British coal abroad fell dramatically. Boom turned to bust. Suddenly, many of those who had worked in coal mining, shipbuilding and engineering, found themselves unemployed and poverty stricken. In 1936 some two hundred representatives of the Jarrow community marched to London to draw attention to their plight. It was one of many protest marches that took place during the Depression years of the inter-war period.

Today, the closure of shipyards, engineering works and coal mines has resulted in initiatives to attract new industries to the North-East. In the process, surface evidence of many colliery sites has been swept away. Today, ironically, there are more traces of Roman occupation in Northumbria than there are of the far more recent coal-mining industry, in which tens of thousands of people were formerly employed.

KILLHOPE LEAD MINING CENTRE, WEARDALE

In 1853, when lead mining in Weardale was at its peak, W. B. Lead (owned by W. B. Beaumont) opened the Park Level Mine at Killhope, near the head of the valley. As each gang or 'partnership' (usually made up of four men) was paid only for the amount of ore they produced, most of the miners had to feed themselves and their families by farming – not made easy by the poor soil and harsh climate of the high Pennine terrain. Furthermore, all the farms in the Killhope valley were owned by W. B. Beaumont, to whom the miner-farmers had to pay rent. They also had to buy their own candles, gunpowder and tools. Life was difficult and dangerous. Those miners not killed or maimed by accidents or explosions, risked early death through lung disease. Some were forced to give up work before the age of forty, while most were considered old men at fifty-five. The mine was taken over by the Weardale Lead Company in 1883 and finally closed during the First World War. Today, the Park Level Mine, with its giant waterwheel and underground workings, has been restored and is open to the public.

SMELT MILL FLUE, LINTZGARTH

Standing in forlorn isolation near Lintzgarth, about one-and-a-half kms (one mile) west of the lead-mining village of Rookhope, is all that remains of a stone viaduct built to carry a smelt mill flue across the Rookhope Burn valley. From the viaduct, the flue – carrying poisonous fumes from the lead-smelting process – headed north-west, climbing gently up the slopes of Redburn Common for almost three kms (two miles), before ending in a vertical stack or chimney. For a short while, two smelt mills operated in the valley at Lintzgarth: the earliest was probably built in the mid-seventeenth century, whilst its replacement dated from the 1730s. Extracted ore was brought from neighbouring mines to be smelted at Lintzgarth, after which most of the finished lead was transported overland (first by packhorse and later by railway) to Tyneside for export to London and Europe. When the Lintzgarth mill was finally closed and demolished in 1919, Weardale ore was taken directly to Tyneside for smelting there.

CAULDRON SNOUT, COW GREEN RESERVOIR

At Cauldron Snout (as well as at High and Low Force, further down the valley) the River Tees pours over an outcrop of Whin Sill – a hard, crystalline, igneous rock, formed after molten magma from deep within the earth had been forced up between layers of sedimentary rocks and solidified. The amount of water cascading down the sixty-metre (200-foot) long staircase of rock at Cauldron Snout is controlled by sluices in the massive concrete dam of the Cow Green Reservoir (opened in 1971). Indeed, the main purpose of the reservoir, unlike those in Baldersdale and Lunedale, is to regulate water down the Tees in accordance with consumer demand. Water from Kielder Water can also be fed into the Tees at Eggleston (near Lunedale) by means of an underground aqueduct. The Widdybank Fell Nature Trail, established in 1963, runs from the Cow Green carpark to Cauldron Snout. Although grazed by sheep and managed as a grouse moor, the reserve is noted for its unusual geology, including 'sugar' limestone, and its rare alpine plants.

HARWOOD, UPPER TEESDALE

Although the main industries of Upper Teesdale are now farming and tourism, the area was once noted for lead mining. Evidence of the ore's extraction can even be found in the remote, five-km (three-mile) long valley of the Harwood Beck (a tributary of the Tees). Before mining ceased in the early twentieth century, the men of the scattered village of Harwood found work in the Lady Rake Mine at the head of the dale. They were also smallholders, growing hay in the valley bottom and grazing sheep higher up the fellsides. In *Teesdale*, first published in 1947, Douglas M. Ramsden recorded that, in order to buy the necessities that a farm cannot provide, the inhabitants of Harwood made the journey to Middleton, some sixteen kms (ten miles) distant, in 'a battered old motor-bus', known as the 'Teesdale Queen'. The journey, made on Tuesdays and Saturdays, was a 'social occasion', during which the passengers, who knew each other, exchanged gossip and caught up on news. In the evening the bus would be full of youngsters going to the pictures or a dance at Middleton.

GRASSHOLME RESERVOIR, LUNEDALE

From its source on the uninhabited Pennine wilderness of Lune Forest, the River Lune flows eastward for almost nineteen kms (twelve miles) to join the Tees, near Middleton-in-Teesdale. In 1884, due to a massive increase in demand for water from the growing towns of Middlesbrough and Stockton, work began on building the Hury Reservoir in Baldersdale (the valley immediately south of Lunedale). This was followed by the construction of the Blackton Reservoir, completed in 1896 (also in Baldersdale). Work on the Grassholme Reservoir, in lower Lunedale, began in 1910. It was not finally completed, however, until 1924, when Grassholme was linked to Hury by a tunnel. Between 1950 and 1970, industrial Teesside's insatiable appetite for water led to the building of three massive new reservoirs: Balderhead in Baldersdale, Selset in Lunedale and Cow Green at the head of Teesdale. Water from the five reservoirs in Lunedale and Baldersdale is cleaned at the Lartington Treatment Works before being piped to consumers as far away as Cleveland.

HIGH FORCE, TEESDALE

Plunging twenty-one metres (seventy feet) over an outcrop of the Great Whin Sill, eight kms (five miles) upstream of Middleton-in-Teesdale, High Force is reputed to be the biggest waterfall in England in terms of water flow. However, since the construction of the Cow Green Reservoir in the late 1960s, the amount of water pouring over the falls can be largely controlled. Tradition says that when J. M. W. Turner was sketching 'High Force' (or 'Fall of the Tees') in 1816, he was so absorbed in his work that he was overtaken by darkness. After getting completely lost and in very real danger of losing his life, he was eventually rescued by a passing shepherd. At the time of Turner's visit, the water flowed over the dolerite cliff in two channels, one on either side of the central rock bastion. Today, this only happens after periods of particularly heavy rain. Turner also sketched the 'Chain Bridge Over the Tees', or the Wynch Bridge, reputed to be the oldest suspension bridge in Britain. The present structure, which crosses the gorge just below Low Force, dates from 1830.

RIVER TEES, FROM HIGH FORCE

Rising on the slopes of Cross Fell – at 2,930 feet (893 metres) the highest point in the Pennines – the River Tees flows in an easterly direction for some 120 kms (seventy-five miles) to enter the North Sea beyond Middlesbrough. Between Cow Green Reservoir and Barnard Castle the river passes through the upland valley of Teesdale, the most northerly of the Yorkshire Dales until the revision of county boundaries in 1974. The largest settlement in the dale, Middleton-in-Teesdale, was transformed from an agricultural community into a prosperous village during the nineteenth century by the Quaker-owned London Lead Company. Although the village became the northern headquarters of its operations in 1880, the company ceased mining in Teesdale in 1905, forcing many families to leave in search of work elsewhere. Mining in Teesdale, however, was not restricted to lead, the extraction of which dates back to the Middle Ages and possibly even Roman times. The area was also an important producer of iron ore, zinc and barytes and, to a lesser extent, fluorspar.

BALDERSDALE, NEAR HURY RESERVOIR

During May and June in Teesdale and its tributary valley, Baldersdale, the hay meadows that have been traditionally managed (farmed without the use of artificial fertilizers, herbicides or re-seeding) are ablaze with a colourful sward of plants and grasses. In 1988 Durham Wildlife Trust purchased two hay meadows and a pasture field from Hannah Hauxwell, who became a national celebrity after appearing in the Yorkshire Television documentary *Too Long a Winter* (first broadcast in 1973). At the time, she was living alone – with no electricity and no water on tap – in the remote Baldersdale farm of Low Birk Hatt on the north bank of the Blackton Reservoir. Failing strength forced her to sell up and leave the valley, where she had lived since the age of three. As she never ploughed or used artificial chemicals, her fields (now Hannah's Meadow Nature Reserve and a Site of Special Scientific Interest) support a rich diversity of plants and wildlife. The eighteenth-century barn has been restored and is now a Visitor Centre.

BARNARD CASTLE

Having been granted lands in Teesdale by William Rufus in 1095, Guy de Baliol erected a small earth and timber fortification high on a cliff overlooking the fast-flowing River Tees. His nephew, Bernard de Baliol I, succeeded to the estate in about 1125 and, in addition to replacing the small fortress with a large castle of stone, he established a town outside the walls. Like the castle, the town came to be named after him. Apart from a few short interruptions, the Baliol family held the castle until 1296 when King Edward I captured John Baliol (crowned King of Scotland in 1292) and confiscated his English estates. Ownership of the castle was granted to Guy de Beauchamp, Earl of Warwick, in 1307 and it remained in his family for almost two centuries. From 1481 until 1603 it was a Crown possession, despite being briefly captured by Catholic rebels in 1569. In 1630 the building was partly demolished by Sir Henry Vane to provide materials for the rebuilding of his main residence, Raby Castle. The impressive remains of Barnard Castle are now in the care of English Heritage.

THE BOWES MUSEUM, BARNARD CASTLE

On the eastern outskirts of the market town of Barnard Castle, the Bowes Museum – a huge and spectacular purpose-built edifice in the style of a French château – was named after its founders, John and Josephine Bowes, both of whom died before it was opened to the public in 1892. Born in 1811, John was the illegitimate son of the 10th Earl of Strathmore, whose ancient family seat was at nearby Streatlam Castle (now demolished). From the seventeenth century, the family's wealth was based on mining and transporting coal. Although John did not succeed to the Strathmore title, he did inherit the Durham estates and the family stud. He married Josephine Coffin-Chevallier, a Parisian actress, in 1852. The couple began accumulating art, antiques and ceramics to furnish their two homes (Streatlam Castle and Château du Barry, near Paris). As their collection grew, so did the notion of building a museum in which to house their treasures. Today, Bowes Museum, set in landscaped gardens, is in the care of Durham County Council.

BOWES CASTLE

The Roman road from *Eboracum* (York) to *Luguvalium* (Carlisle) crossed the Pennines by way of the Stainmore Pass, the eastern approach to which was guarded by the fort of *Lavatris* (Bowes), on the River Greta; while the western side was protected by *Verteris* (Brough). Today the north-east corner of the almost four-acre rectangular site at Bowes is occupied by the parish church of St Giles, dating from Norman times and constructed with stone from the Roman buildings. In the north-west corner are the ruins of the castle keep built for Henry II between 1171 and 1187. The castle was besieged and captured in 1322 and by 1341 it was reported to be in a bad state of disrepair. Much of its stone was also plundered for building material in the seventeenth century. The castle remains are now in the care of English Heritage. In 1838 Charles Dickens visited Bowes to investigate rumours of boys being cruelly treated by William Shaw, the headmaster of the boarding-school. Dotheboys Hall, run by Wackford Squeers, in *Nicholas Nickleby* was apparently based on Shaw's academy.

EGGLESTONE ABBEY

On the southern banks of the River Tees, just over one-and-a-half kms (one mile) south-east of Barnard Castle, the abbey of St Mary & St John the Baptist at Egglestone was founded at the close of the twelfth century by Ralph de Multon for a community of Premonstratensian canons from Easby Abbey, near Richmond. Known as 'white canons', because of the colour of their habits, the monks combined a life of prayer and discipline (based on the Cistercian rule of austerity) with work as parish priests serving local communities. The first English house of the Order (all of which were abbeys) was founded at Newsham, north-west of Grimsby, in 1143. Egglestone, which was never very important, suffered so severely from financial difficulties that at one stage it was almost reduced in status to a priory. Like many other religious houses in Northumbria, Egglestone also suffered at the hands of Scottish and English marauders. After its dissolution in 1540, the north and east ranges of the abbey were converted into a manorial hall. The abbey ruins are now in the care of English Heritage.

DURHAM CATHEDRAL AND RIVER WEAR

Standing side by side on a steep rocky peninsular – almost islanded by the River Wear – the Norman cathedral and castle dominate the ancient city of Durham. The first church on the cathedral site was built of timber in 995 by a community of monks, originally from Lindisfarne. Containing the body of St Cuthbert and the head of St Oswald (relics dating from the seventh century), the building was soon replaced by the *Alba Ecclesia* (White Church). In 998, however, work began on a new stone church, the *Ecclesia Major*. After the Norman Conquest, Walcher became the first Norman Bishop of Durham, and from 1074 acted as Earl of Northumbria until he was killed in a riot in 1080. In 1092 the *Ecclesia Major* was pulled down to build the present Romanesque cathedral. Today, the relics of both St Cuthbert and St Oswald lie under a plain marble slab behind the High Altar. The cathedral also contains the bones of the Venerable Bede, which were brought to Durham in about 1022. Situated below the two massive west towers of the cathedral is the Old Fulling Mill.

GATEHOUSE, DURHAM CASTLE

Occupying the site of an earlier fortification, the first Norman castle at Durham was built in about 1072 by the Anglo-Saxon Waltheof, Earl of Northumbria. After Waltheof's execution for treason in 1076, William the Conqueror gave custody of the fortress to Walcher, Bishop of Durham. Thereafter, during the medieval period, it was the stronghold and palace of the powerful warrior Prince Bishops, who ruled the 'County Palatinate of Durham' as a virtually independent state, with their own army, their own judges and even their own mint. Although most of their powers had been removed by the end of the sixteenth century, they retained certain independent privileges and revenues until 1836 – the year the last of the Prince Bishops, William van Mildert, died. Shortly after, the castle became the home of the university, founded in 1832 by the Bishop and the Chapter of the Cathedral. The Gatehouse, dating from Norman times, was altered in the sixteenth century, and then 'romanticized' by James Wyatt at the end of the eighteenth.

FINCHALE PRIORY

On the south bank of the River Wear, some five kms (three miles) north-east of Durham, Finchale Priory owes its origins to a vision which led St Godric to the area in about 1110. Here, after some forty years as a much-travelled merchant, sailor and adventurer (which included several pilgrimages abroad), he retired to live as a hermit. The site he initially chose was about one-and-a-half kms (one mile) upstream of the place now occupied by the priory ruins (and to where he moved in 1115). Godric died in 1170, at the alleged age of 105, and was buried in the stone chapel built especially for him. The property remained a hermitage until 1196, when it became a Benedictine priory dependent on Durham. The Cathedral's sacrist, Thomas, was appointed Finchale's first prior. Although Godric's tomb attracted countless pilgrims, the priory buildings were not begun until about 1237. Unusually, from the fourteenth century until its dissolution, Finchale became a rest centre for Durham monks needing a short break. The ruins are now in the care of English Heritage.

SAXON CHURCH, ESCOMB

Surrounded by a twentieth-century housing estate, one-and-a-half kms (one mile) or so west of Bishop Auckland, the church at Escomb is one of the most complete Anglo-Saxon churches in England. Thought to date from the seventh century, the building contains stones from the Roman fort at *Vinovia* (Binchester) – located just north of Bishop Auckland. Indeed, the chancel arch itself may have been reassembled from a Roman archway. The jambs by which it is supported were constructed in the 'long and short' style, whereby large slabs of stone were laid alternately horizontally and vertically. Behind the altar is a stone cross of the Anglo-Saxon period (originally either part of a standing cross or a grave-marker). A second cross, suggesting a Celtic-Irish influence, can be found inscribed on the wall behind the pulpit. In 1863, when a new church (demolished in 1971) was built in the parish, the Anglo-Saxon building was reduced to the status of a chapel. It regained its status of parish church in 1970, having undergone restoration.

ST MARY'S CHURCH, SEAHAM

In January 1815, when Lord Byron married Anne Isabella Milbanke in an upstairs room of her home, Seaham Hall, and not in the ancient church of St Mary, it was seen by the villagers as an ill omen. They were proved right for, shortly after the birth of their daughter, Ada, the marriage ended. Byron left England for Europe in 1816, never to return. What the villagers did not foresee, however, was that their homes were also doomed. In 1821 Byron's relative, Charles William Stewart (later Vane), 3rd Marquess of Londonderry, purchased the Seaham estate from the Milbankes in order to build a harbour for shipping out coal from the family's Rainton pits, a few miles inland. In the process, every building in Seaham, apart from the church, vicarage and Hall, was demolished. The first stone of the harbour was laid in a ceremony attended by some seven thousand people on 28 November 1828. Three collieries were subsequently opened within a three-km (two-mile) radius of the harbour (Seaham, Vane Tempest and Dawdon). All have now closed.

PENSHAW MONUMENT

Prominently sited on the top of a hill, five kms (three miles) north-east of Lambton Castle, the Penshaw Monument was erected in 1844 to commemorate the radical statesman John George Lambton, 1st Earl of Durham, who died in 1840. Its design was based on the Temple of Theseum in Athens, although half its size. According to legend, the countryside around Penshaw was once terrorized by a hideous monster called the Lambton Worm. Apparently, the creature (as a tiny worm) was caught in the River Wear by John, the young heir of Lambton Castle, and thrown in to a nearby well. The years passed and John went on Crusade to the Holy Land. On his return, he was horrified to find that the tiny worm had grown into an enormous beast, with a ravenous appetite that included swallowing small children alive. Although John managed to kill it with the help of a wise old witch, he failed to obey her strict conditions and brought a curse down on the Lambton family – that for nine generations none of its chiefs would die in their bed.

ROKER PIER, SUNDERLAND HARBOUR

Formerly a major coal-exporting port and shipbuilding town, Sunderland – straddling both sides of the mouth of the River Wear – became a city in 1992, four years after the controversial closure of its last shipyard. Originally the port, on the south side of the river, belonged to (Monk)Wearmouth Abbey, situated on the north (from which it was 'sundered'). During medieval times, it was owned by the bishops of Durham (hence the name of its neighbouring and once larger settlement, Bishopwearmouth). Sunderland grew rapidly from the end of the sixteenth century, despite fierce competition from the far wealthier and more powerful port of Newcastle-upon-Tyne. Rivalry between the two towns intensified during the Civil War when Sunderland sided with the Parliamentarians and Newcastle with the Royalists. By supporting the winning cause, Sunderland finally broke Newcastle's monopolistic hold on the export of coal in the area. The harbour's outer piers were rebuilt at the end of the nineteenth century – the North, or Roker Pier, between 1885 and 1903.

ST PETER'S CHURCH, MONKWEARMOUTH

After making several pilgrimages to Rome, during which time he abandoned his secular career to become a monk, the Northumbrian nobleman, Benedict Biscop, founded the monastery of St Peter at Wearmouth (Monkwearmouth) in 674, becoming its first abbot. The site, on the north side of the River Wear at Sunderland, was granted to the monks by Ecgfrith, King of Northumbria. According to Bede, Benedict brought builders from Europe to teach the brothers how 'to construct a church of stone after the Roman fashion'. The abbot also enriched the monastery with paintings and books collected during his travels on the Continent. Together with Jarrow (to which it was inextricably linked), the monastery became one of the most influential centres of Christianity and learning in Europe. Like Jarrow, it was abandoned in the ninth century, refounded shortly after the Norman Conquest, and was made a dependent cell of Durham in 1083. Today, all that remains of the Anglo-Saxon monastery are large sections of stonework incorporated into the later St Peter's Church.

WHITBURN WINDMILL

Occupying a hilltop site overlooking the village of Whitburn and the limestone cliffs of the south Tyneside coast, is a three-storey stone tower windmill, once used to grind corn from local farms. Built in 1796, after the previous mill on the site had blown down, it is the oldest of the three surviving tower windmills in South Tyneside (the others are at Cleadon and West Boldon). After it ceased working in the mid-nineteenth century, the wooden cap, sails and fantail rotted and decayed. Apart from being used as a lookout post during the Second World War, the tower stood as a roofless, empty shell until it was restored in 1990–91. From the 1870s, the cliffs north of the windmill (near the Souter lighthouse) were occupied by Whitburn Colliery and the houses of the pitmen and their families in Marsden village. Since the closure of the colliery in 1968, virtually all evidence of its existence, including the nine terraces in which the miners lived for almost a century, together with their gardens and allotments, has been cleared away.

SOUTER LIGHTHOUSE, WHITBURN

For centuries the submerged rocks off Whitburn and Marsden were particularly dangerous to shipping. During the nineteenth century, the growth of heavy industry in the area around Newcastle and Sunderland brought a massive increase in coastal traffic. In 1870, the year after some twenty vessels had foundered between the mouths of the rivers Tyne and Wear, work started on building the Souter lighthouse. Designed by Sir James Douglass, Chief Engineer to Trinity House, it was opened in 1871 and was the first shore-based lighthouse to be powered by alternating electric current. Originally, it was planned to erect the lighthouse on Souter Point (just over a kilometre to the south), but it was deemed that the light would be seen more clearly if it was built on the higher cliffs of Lizard Point. The name 'Souter', however, was retained to avoid confusion with the lighthouse on the Lizard in Cornwall. The lighthouse ceased operation in 1988 (apart from an automatic radio beacon) and is now in the care of the National Trust.

SOUTH TYNESIDE COAST, WHITBURN

The limestone cliffs and isolated rock stacks and arches along the coast between South Shields and Whitburn Bay provide safe nesting ledges for a large number of seabirds, including kittiwakes, razorbills and guillemots. In winter, turnstones and purple sandpipers may be found feeding along the rocky shore, whilst black redstarts and warblers often frequent the disused Trow Quarry during times of migration. Situated at the northern extremity of the National Trust's property of the Leas, Trow Quarry provided limestone hardcore for the construction of the Tyne Piers in the latter half of the nineteenth century. In 1887, an experimental 'disappearing gun' was set up on Trow Rock, which could be lowered into a hidden chamber set in the rock. Although the weapon (a new breech-loading coastal defence gun) and its mounting were removed soon after the trial period, a static replica was erected on the site in 1989. 'Concretions' – round ball-like structures – can also be found in areas of the cliffs where layers of brown crystalline limestone occurs.

THE LEAS, SOUTH SHIELDS

The Leas, the five-km (three-mile) stretch of coast between Trow Point and Lizard Point, covering almost 300 acres of grassland, cliffs and foreshore, is owned by the National Trust and has been designated a Site of Special Scientific Interest (SSSI). The cliffs, composed of magnesian limestone of the Permian period (formed about 245 million years ago), are noted for displaying classic examples of coastal erosion, including natural rock arches, stacks, caves and ledges. The most famous rock formation (until it collapsed in February 1996) was the massive arch of Marsden Rock. The smallest of the two stacks that remained was subsequently blown up for safety reasons. Marsden Grotto, at the foot of the cliffs near Marsden Rock, was originally a natural cave used by smugglers. The first person to make the cave his permanent home was 'Jack the Blaster' (so-named because he used explosives to enlarge it). He moved in with his wife in 1782. His home developed into the present Marsden Grotto public house and restaurant.

TYNE BRIDGE, NEWCASTLE-UPON-TYNE

The most famous of the six bridges spanning the river in the heart of Newcastle-upon-Tyne is the Tyne Bridge, opened in 1928. Designed by the firm of Mott Hay & Anderson and constructed by Dorman Long & Co., the riveted steel arched bridge has become an enduring symbol of Tyneside. The arch itself has a span of 162 metres (531 feet), while the suspended road deck is twenty-six metres (eighty-four feet) above the river. At the time of its completion it was the largest single-span road bridge in Britain. A short distance upriver is the low-level Tyne Swing Road Bridge, opened in 1876. It replaced Mylne's nine-arch stone bridge of 1781, which prevented large vessels from reaching W. G. Armstrong's Elswick Works. The nearby High Level Bridge was designed by Robert Stephenson (with T. E. Harrison). Opened in 1849, it carried both road and rail across the Tyne. Between the High Level Bridge and the King Edward VII Rail Bridge of 1906 is the Queen Elizabeth II Metro Bridge of 1980. Further upriver is the Redheugh Road Bridge, opened in 1983.

BLACK GATE & CATHEDRAL, NEWCASTLE-UPON-TYNE

Dating from the mid-thirteenth century, the Black Gate (surmounted by a small seventeenth-century brick house) was erected to guard the northern approach to the stone castle built by Henry II in 1168–78. Most of the castle and town walls were demolished during the reconstruction of the city centre in the eighteenth and nineteenth centuries, when Newcastle became a major coal-exporting port. During Victorian times, the Black Gate and the Castle Keep were separated by a railway viaduct. The first Norman fortification, or 'New Castle', was founded in 1080 by Robert Curthose, eldest son of William the Conqueror, to protect the lowest bridging point of the Tyne. In Roman times the site was occupied by the fort of *Pons Aelius* (named after the nearby bridge it was designed to protect). Later, the site was an Anglo-Saxon cemetery. St Nicholas' Cathedral, its tower crowned by a lantern and spire, dates from the fourteenth and fifteenth centuries. The parish church became a cathedral when the town was made a city in 1882.

PRIORY & CHURCH, JARROW

The monastery of St Paul at Jarrow was first founded in 681 by St Benedict Biscop, who also founded the monastery of St Peter at Wearmouth (Monkwearmouth), eleven kms (seven miles) distant. Both houses, essentially one monastery, were associated with St Bede (673–735), the celebrated scholar and historian, who entered Wearmouth at the age of seven and moved to Jarrow soon after its foundation. Although he was buried in St Paul's church, his bones are now in Durham. By the middle of the ninth century the monastery had been abandoned. It was refounded as a priory for Benedictine monks in 1074 by Aldwin, Prior of Winchcombe, Gloucestershire. In 1083, however, it became a dependent cell of Durham, housing only a few monks. The present parish church, which remained in use after the dissolution and destruction of the priory buildings, preserves the chancel of the seventh-century monastic church. It was built with Roman stone – possibly from Wallsend or South Shields (*Arbeia*). Nearby is Bede's World, 'the Museum of Early Medieval Northumbria'.

TYNEMOUTH PRIORY

The earliest monastery to stand on the rocky headland north of the River Tyne, was founded some time before the middle of the seventh century. According to tradition, St Oswin, King of Deira, was buried there in 651 after being killed on the orders of his cousin, Oswy, King of Northumbria. The murdered Osred, King of Northumbria, was also buried at Tynemouth in 792. In 875, after regular raids, the monastery was finally destroyed by the Danes. It was refounded in 1085 for Benedictine monks from St Albans Abbey, Hertfordshire, by Robert de Mowbray, Earl of Northumberland. After Malcolm III, King of Scotland, was killed at Alnwick in 1093, his body was interred in the priory church. It was later moved to Dunfermline Abbey. The priory stood within the fortifications of Tynemouth Castle, also founded by Mowbray. After the Dissolution, the site became part of Henry VIII's coastal defence scheme. The ruins of both castle and priory are now in the care of English Heritage. The lighthouse in the photograph stands on the South Tyne Pier, South Shields.

ARBEIA ROMAN FORT, SOUTH SHIELDS

As part of their frontier defence system the Romans built the fort of *Arbeia* (South Shields) on a low headland overlooking the mouth of the River Tyne. Situated six kms (four miles) downstream of Wallsend, it was an important military supply base, especially during Emperor Septimius Severus' campaigns into Scotland from AD 208. The earliest visible remains of a fort on the site probably date from approximately AD 160, when Hadrian's Wall was re-occupied (it had been abandoned when the frontier was moved north by the construction of the Antonine Wall). In the early third century, when it was converted into a supply base, the fort was extended in area from some four acres to just over five. Most of the buildings inside the walls were demolished and replaced by stone granaries. Severus' death at York in 211 brought an end to the Scottish campaigns and, instead of providing stores for a great army, *Arbeia* became a supply base for the garrisons and forts of Rome's northern frontier. The west gate reconstruction was built on the original foundations in 1986.

PHOTOGRAPHIC NOTES

Hﾉﾉigh summer, approaching noon, and my body was telling me to stop and take refreshment. I had been working since dawn with few other thoughts than those associated with taking photographs. The sky was rich blue and cloudless, as it had been all morning. The day had started warm and increased so much in temperature that it seemed more like the Mediterranean than the north-easternmost corner of England. As I wasn't far from Bamburgh Castle, I turned my camper van into a narrow lane that led to the beach. It would be the perfect place to stop for lunch and a short siesta before I resumed work. From my elevated parking spot, high up in the sand dunes, I could see the magnificent citadel of Bamburgh Castle, together with mile after mile of golden sand and, beyond, the Farne Islands, scene of many a shipwreck. Eventually, I settled back into a comfortable deckchair with George, my border collie, stretched out at my feet. From my viewpoint, an impressive sweep of sea and sand lay before me. The beach seemed totally deserted. Looking through the binoculars, however, I managed to count five people in almost as many miles. It was incredible, and seemed an undiscovered landscape. At this time of the year, Yorkshire to the south and the Lake District to the west would have been heaving with people. But here, in Northumbria, I was almost alone – and enjoying the most perfect weather.

If there was just one scene that could sum up the recurring experiences I enjoyed whilst working in Northumbria, this was it. The sunny weather (which was most unexpected as I usually had to battle against the elements); the amazing heritage (Bamburgh Castle, a powerful reminder that the Borderlands were in a state of turmoil for centuries); the extraordinary beauty of the landscape (not just on the coast, but inland, on hilltop, moorland and valley); and the mystery of the place (where solitude and atmosphere can so readily be found when required). Northumbria is indeed a land apart. Somewhere special; unique even. Photographers who love the English landscape should visit this glorious region soon. You will not be disappointed. The cameras used were: Hasselblad 503CX with 50mm, 80mm and 150mm lenses; and Nikon F3 with 28mmPC, 35mm and 85mm lenses. The film was Fuji.

ROB TALBOT

ENGLISH HERITAGE

HEAD OFFICE
Savile Row
London W1X 1AB
Tel: (0171) 973 3000

HISTORIC PROPERTIES NORTH
Bessie Surtees House
41–44 Sandhill
Newcastle-upon-Tyne NE1 3JF
Tel: (0191) 261 1585

AYDON CASTLE
Corbridge
Northumberland NE45 5PU
Tel: (01434) 632 450
Open April to end October
daily.

BARNARD CASTLE
Castle House
Barnard Castle
County Durham DL12 9AT
Tel: (01833) 638 212
Open April to end October
daily; November to March,
Wednesdays to Sundays.
Closed 24–26 December.

BELSAY HALL, CASTLE
& GARDENS
Belsay
Ponteland
Northumberland NE20 0DX
Tel: (01661) 881 636
Open daily throughout the year.
Closed 24–26 December.

BERWICK BARRACKS
The Parade
Berwick-upon-Tweed
Northumberland TD15 1DF
Tel: (01289) 304 493
Open Easter to end October
daily; November to March,
Wednesdays to Sundays.
Closed 24–26 December.

BESSIE SURTEES HOUSE
41 Sandhill
Newcastle-upon-Tyne NE1 3JF
Tel: (0191) 261 1585
Open weekdays only. Closed
Bank Holidays.

BRINKBURN PRIORY
Longframlington
Morpeth
Northumberland NE65 8AR
Tel: (01665) 570 628
Open April to end October.

CARLISLE CASTLE
Carlisle
Cumbria CA2 8UR
Tel: (01228) 591 922
Open daily throughout the year.
Closed 24–26 December.

ETAL CASTLE
Etal
near Cornhill-on-Tweed
Northumberland TD12 4TN
Tel: (01890) 820 332
Open April to end October
daily.

FINCHALE PRIORY
Brasside
Newton Hall
County Durham DH1 5SH
Tel: (0191) 386 3828
Open April to end September
daily.

HADRIAN'S WALL:
CORBRIDGE ROMAN SITE
Corbridge
Northumberland NE45 5NT
Tel: (01434) 632 349
Open April to end October
daily; November to March,
Wednesdays to Sundays.
Closed 24–26 December.

LANERCOST PRIORY
near Brampton
Cumbria CA8 2HQ
Tel: (01697) 73030
Open April to end October daily.

LINDISFARNE PRIORY
Holy Island
Berwick-upon-Tweed
Northumberland TD15 2RX
Tel: (01289) 389 200
Open daily throughout the year,
except 24–26 December.

NORHAM CASTLE
Norham
Berwick-upon-Tweed
Northumberland TD15 1DF
Tel: (01289) 382 329
Open April to end October daily.

PRUDHOE CASTLE
Prudhoe
Northumberland NE42 6NA
Tel: (01661) 833 459
Open April to end September
daily.

TYNEMOUTH PRIORY & CASTLE
Tynemouth
North Shields
Tyne & Wear NE30 4BZ
Tel: (0191) 257 1090
Open April to end October
daily; November to March,
Wednesdays to Sundays.
Closed 24–26 December.

WARKWORTH CASTLE
Warkworth
Morpeth
Northumberland NE66 0UJ
Tel: (01665) 711 423
Open daily throughout the year,
except 24–26 December.

NATIONAL TRUST

HEAD OFFICE
36 Queen Anne's Gate
London SW1H 9AS
Tel: (0171) 222 9251

NORTHUMBRIA REGIONAL
OFFICE
Scots' Gap
Morpeth
Northumberland NE61 4EG
Tel: (01670) 774 691

CRAGSIDE HOUSE,
GARDEN & GROUNDS
Rothbury
Morpeth
Northumberland NE65 7PX
Tel: (01669) 620 333/620 266
House & Garden open April to
end October daily, Tuesdays to
Sundays & Bank Holiday
Mondays. Grounds open
November to mid-December,
Tuesdays, Saturdays & Sundays.

DUNSTANBURGH CASTLE
Craster
Northumberland
Tel: (01665) 576 231
Open April to October daily;
November to March,
Wednesdays to Sundays.
Closed 24–26 December.

GEORGE STEPHENSON'S
BIRTHPLACE
Wylam
Northumberland NE41 8BP
Tel: (01661) 853 457
Open April to end October,
Thursdays, Saturdays & Sundays.

HADRIAN'S WALL
& HOUSESTEADS FORT
Haydon Bridge
Hexham
Northumberland NE47 6NN
Tel: (01434) 344 363
Open daily throughout the year,
except 24–26 December.

LINDISFARNE CASTLE
Holy Island
Berwick-upon-Tweed
Northumberland TD15 2SH
Tel: (01289) 89244
Open April to end October,
Saturdays to Thursdays & Good
Fridays.

SOUTER LIGHTHOUSE
Coast Road
Whitburn
Sunderland SR6 7NR
Tel: (0191) 529 3161
Open April to end October,
Saturdays to Thursdays
& Good Fridays.

WALLINGTON HOUSE
& GARDEN
Cambo
Morpeth
Northumberland NE61 4AR
Tel: (01670) 774 283
House open April to end
October, Wednesdays to
Mondays. Gardens open daily
throughout the year.

NORTHUMBERLAND
NATIONAL PARK

PARK OFFICE
Eastburn
South Park
Hexham
Northumberland NE36 1BS
Tel: (01434) 605 555

MISCELLANEOUS

ALNWICK CASTLE
Estate Office
Alnwick
Northumberland NE66 1NQ
Tel: (01665) 510 777
Open Easter to end September
daily.

APPLEBY CASTLE
Appleby-in-Westmorland
Cumbria CA16 6XH
Tel: (017683) 51402
Open April to end October daily.

ARBEIA ROMAN FORT MUSEUM
Baring Street
South Shields NE33 2BB
Tel: (0191) 456 8740
Open daily throughout the year.
September to March,
closed Sundays & 25–26
December & 1 January.

BAMBURGH CASTLE
Bamburgh
Northumberland NE69 7DF
Tel: (01668) 214 208
Open April to end October daily.

BIRDOSWALD ROMAN FORT
Gilsland
Carlisle
Cumbria CA6 7DD
Tel: (016977) 47602
Open April to end October
daily.

THE BOWES MUSEUM
Barnard Castle
County Durham DL12 8NP
Tel: (01833) 690 606
Open daily throughout the year,
except 25–26 December
& 1 January.

CHILLINGHAM CASTLE
Chillingham
Alnwick
Northumberland NE66 5NJ
Tel: (01668) 215 359
Open Easter; May, June &
September, Wednesdays to
Mondays; July & August daily.

DURHAM CASTLE
Palace Green
Durham DH1 3RW
Tel: (0191) 374 3863
Open (guided tours only) daily
at certain times throughout the
year. (Please ring before your
visit.)

KILLHOPE LEAD MINING CENTRE
Killhope
Upper Weardale
County Durham
Tel: (01388) 537 505 or
(0191) 383 3354 (24 hours)
Open April to end October
daily; November, Sundays only.

NENTHEAD MINES HERITAGE
CENTRE
Nenthead
near Alston
Cumbria CA9 3PD
Tel: (01434) 382 037
Open April to end October daily.

PRESTON TOWER
Chathill
Northumberland NE67 5DH
Tel: (01665) 589 227
Open daily all year during
daylight hours.

RABY CASTLE
Staindrop
Darlington
County Durham DL2 3AY
Tel: (01833) 660 202
Open Easter & Bank Holidays;
May & June, Wednesdays &
Sundays; July & September,
Mondays to Fridays & Sundays.

ROMAN ARMY MUSEUM
Greenhead
Northumberland CA6 7JB
Tel: (016977) 47485
Open mid-February to
mid-November daily.

ST PAUL'S MONASTERY & BEDE'S
WORLD MUSEUM
Church Bank
Jarrow
Tyne & Wear NE32 3DY
Tel: (0191) 489 2106

Monastery ruins open at any
reasonable time. Museum open
Tuesdays to Sundays throughout
the year & Bank Holidays.
Closed Christmas & New Year.

SEATON DELAVAL HALL
Seaton Sluice
Whitley Bay
Northumberland NE26 4QR
Tel: (0191) 237 3040/237 1493
Open May Bank Holiday
Sundays & Mondays; June,
Wednesdays & Sundays; July &
August, Tuesdays, Wednesdays,
Sundays & Bank Holidays.

VINDOLANDA ROMAN FORT
& CHESTERHOLM MUSEUM
Bardon Mill
Hexham
Northumberland NE47 7JN
Tel: (01434) 344 277
Open daily from early February
to mid-November.

BIBLIOGRAPHY

Aubrey, John, *Monumenta Britannica: A Miscellany of British Antiquities* (compiled 1665–93), Dorset Publishing Company, Sherborne, 1980 (1st pub.)

Bates, C. J., *History of Northumberland*, Elliot Stock, London, 1895

Beckensall, Stan, *Prehistoric Rock Motifs of Northumberland* (Vols. 1 & 2), Beckensall, Hexham, 1991 & 1992

Birley, Robin, *The Building of Hadrian's Wall*, Roman Army Museum Publications, Greenhead, 1991

Birley, Robin, *Vindolanda's Roman Records*, Roman Army Museum Publications, Greenhead, 1994

Bowes, Peter, *Picturesque Weardale Revisited*, Weardale Publishing, Bishop Auckland, 1996

Bowes, Peter, *Weardale: Clearing the Forest*, Bowes, 1990

Bowman, Alan K., *Life & Letters on the Roman Frontier*, British Museum Press, London, 1994

Bradley, A. G., *The Romance of Northumberland*, Methuen, London, 1913

Camden, William, *Britannia*, Gibson, London, 1695 (1st pub. 1586)

Charleton, R. J., *History of Newcastle-Upon-Tyne*, Harold Hill, Newcastle-upon-Tyne, 1950

Charlton, Beryl, *The Story of Redesdale*, Northumberland National Park, Hexham, 1986

Charlton, Beryl, *Upper North Tynedale: A Northumbrian Valley & its People*, Northumbrian Water, 1987

Cockcroft, Barry, (Hannah Hauxwell), *Seasons of My Life*, Century Hutchinson, London, 1989

Crow, James, *English Heritage Book of Housesteads*, Batsford, London, 1995

Defoe, Daniel, *A Tour Thro' the Whole Island of Great Britain*, Peter Davies, London, 1927

Durham, Keith, & McBride, Angus, *The Border Reivers*, Osprey, London, 1995

Eastwood, T., *British Regional Geology: Northern England* (3rd ed.), HMSO, London, 1953

Emett, Charlie, *The Eden Way*, Cicerone Press, Milnthorpe, 1990

Fraser, George MacDonald, *The Steel Bonnets: The Story of the Anglo-Scottish Border Reivers*, Barrie & Jenkins, London, 1971

Graham, Frank, *The Old Halls, Houses and Inns of Northumberland*, Frank Graham, Newcastle-upon-Tyne, 1977

Graham, P. Anderson, *Highways & Byways in Northumbria*, Macmillan, London, 1928

A Handbook for Travellers in Durham & Northumberland (2nd ed.), Murray, London, 1873

Hardy, Charles E., *John Bowes & the Bowes Museum*, Frank Graham, Newcastle-upon-Tyne, 1970

Hartley, Brian, & Fitts, Leon, *The Brigantes* (Peoples of Roman Britain series), Sutton, Stroud, 1988

Hartley, Ian, & Brown, Mike, (comps.), *A Celebration of Bridges between the Tweed & the Tees*, Institution of Civil Engineers, Newcastle-upon-Tyne, 1995

Higham, N. J., *The Kingdom of Northumbria: AD 350–1100*, Sutton, Stroud, 1993

Hodgkin, J. E., *Durham* (Little Guides series), Methuen, London, 1913

Hopkins, Tony, *Northumberland National Park*, Webb & Bower, London, 1987

Howitt, William, *Visits to Remarkable Places*, Longmans, Green & Co., London, 1890

Hugill, Robert, *Borderland Castles & Peles*, Burrow, London, 1939

Hunnewell, James F., *The Lands of Scott*, Osgood, Boston, 1871

Hutchinson, William, *The History of the County of Cumberland* (2 Vols.), Jollie, Carlisle, 1794

Hutton, William, *The History of the Roman Wall*, Nichols, Son & Bentley, London, 1813 (1st pub. 1802)

Jenkinson, Henry Irwin, *Practical Guide to Carlisle, Gilsland, Roman Wall, & Neighbourhood*, Stanford, London, 1875

Jervoise, E., *The Ancient Bridges of the North of England*, Architectural Press, London 1931

Johnson, Stephen, *English Heritage Book of Hadrian's Wall*, Batsford, London, 1989

Macaulay, Lord, *The History of England*, Longmans, Green, Reader & Dyer, London, 1880

Mackay, James, *William Wallace: Braveheart*, Mainstream, Edinburgh, 1995

Milburn, T. A., *Life & Times in Weardale 1840–1910*, The Weardale Museum, Ireshopeburn, 1987

Neville, Hastings M., *A Corner in the North: Yesterday and Today with Border Folk*, Reid, Newcastle-upon-Tyne, 1909

Pevsner, Nikolaus, *County Durham* (The Buildings of England series), Penguin Books, Harmondsworth, 1953 (2nd ed. 1983)

Pevsner, Nikolaus, *Cumberland & Westmorland* (The Buildings of England series), Penguin Books, Harmondsworth, 1967

Pevsner, Nikolaus, & Richmond, Ian, *Northumberland* (The Buildings of England series), Penguin Books, Harmondsworth, 1992

Proud, J. Keith, *Charles Dickens in Teesdale*, Discovery Guides, Middleton-in-Teesdale, 1983

Raistrick, Arthur, *Lead Mining in the Yorkshire Dales*, Dalesman Books, Clapham, 1972

Raistrick, Arthur, *The Pennine Dales* (Regions of Britain series), Eyre & Spottiswoode, London, 1968

Ramsden, Douglas M., *Teesdale*, Museum Press, London, 1947

Roberts, Martin, *English Heritage Book of Durham*, Batsford, London, 1994

Scott, Sir Walter, *The Works of Sir Walter Scott*, Wordsworth Editions, Ware, 1995

Sharp, Thomas, *A Shell Guide: Northumberland*, Faber & Faber, London, 1937

Smith, Lucy Toulmin, (ed.), *The Itinerary of John Leland*, Southern Illinois University Press, Carbondale, 1964

Steers, J. A., *The Coastline of England & Wales*, Cambridge University Press, 1969

Terry, Jean F., *Northumberland: Yesterday & Today*, Reid, Newcastle-upon-Tyne, 1913

Thain, Louise M., *'Through the Ages': The Story of Nenthead*, North Pennines Heritage Trust, Alston, 1957

Tomlinson, W. W., *Comprehensive Guide to Northumberland*, Walter Scott Publishing, Newcastle-upon-Tyne, 1888

Walton, Izaak, *The Compleat Angler*, Oxford University Press, 1982 (1st pub. 1653)

Watson, Godfrey, *The Border Reivers*, Hale, London, 1974

White, Walter, *Northumberland & the Border*, Chapman & Hall, London, 1859

Wilson, Keith, & Leathart, Scott, (eds.), *The Keilder Forests*, Forestry Commission, London, 1982

Wilson's Historical, Traditionary, and Imaginative Tales of the Borders and of Scotland (2 Vols), Adam, Gateshead-on-Tyne, n.d.

❧